CW00879820

The **Spirit Level** Delusion

FACT-CHECKING THE LEFT'S NEW THEORY OF EVERYTHING

Christopher **Snowdon**

with a foreword by Patrick Basham

Published in Great Britain in 2010
by Little Dice

Copyright 2010 © Christopher Snowdon

ISBN 978-0-9562265-1-8

All rights reserved.
No part of this publication may be reproduced in any form
without the prior written permission of the author.

Democracy Institute
2nd Floor
145-157 St John Street
London
EC1V 4PY

Little Dice
Trinity Farm, Middleton Quernhow
Ripon, North Yorkshire
HG4 5HX
United Kingdom

www.spiritleveldelusion.com

Cover by Devil's Kitchen Design

Thanks

Sincere thanks to James, Tim, Emma, Chris, Nora, Patrick, Marilyn, Peter and everyone else who contributed thoughts, ideas and assistance in the writing of this book.

Foreword

Christopher Snowdon first appeared on our radar screens at the Democracy Institute when we heard about his seminal volume, *Velvet Glove, Iron Fist: A History of Anti-Smoking*. In addition to being a fascinating read and an insightful critique of the modern anti-smoking movement, Snowdon's ability to put his analytical arms around such a voluminous and controversial topic signalled that this youthful historian had plenty of dry powder remaining in his intellectual arsenal.

Very fortunately for those interested in and concerned about the level of public debate on important economic matters, Snowdon has now turned his keen attention to the even-larger issue of economic policy making. While he is not a trained economist, he is clearly a serious, and a seriously accomplished, economic historian, as both the textual and graphic presentations in this new book attest.

In recent years, anti-capitalist treatises have done very well on the bestseller charts and also atop many a book reviewer's 'Best of the Year' list. The most obvious example of this tendency of book buyers and critics alike to embrace statist economic thinking is *The Spirit Level: Why more equal societies almost always do better*, written by Richard Wilkinson and Kate Pickett. Although Snowdon reserves some of his analytical slings and arrows for several of Wilkinson and Pickett's ideological soul mates, most of his considerable empirical arsenal is unleashed on the arguments presented in *The Spirit Level*.

When Christopher Snowdon first talked about *The Spirit Level* with me, we discussed the book's supposedly avant-garde thesis. Both of us were surprised that such an anachronistic perspective on economic policy could strike so many members of the media and the political class as both new and relevant to our current economic predicament. Crudely stated, Wilkinson and Pickett advocate that the State (or, rather, those Wise Persons who control the levers of State power) play a zero-sum game with our economic lives.

For me, personally, Wilkinson and Pickett's thesis brings back vividly unpleasant memories of an undergraduate year in the mid-1980s that I spent, in part, being taught about socio-economic matters by my sociology tutor, a newly-minted Marxist feminist PhD. She had little tolerance for my 'tax cutting equals economic growth equals more employment' economic model, which she termed, 'An ungodly synthesis of the worst of Reaganism and Thatcherism' (which I thought oddly religious rhetoric for such a fanatical atheist). 'On the contrary, Patrick,' she would inform me, 'you need to get over your fixation with economic growth. Rather than putting all our effort behind growing the economic pie, we should instead limit the pie to its current size, and then focus our energies on the issue of how we shall divide it up.'

There it was: Eighties-style socialist fundamentalism in a nutshell. Two sentences that encapsulated the British Labour Party's economic thinking at the height of the Left's control of the party and at the nadir of the party's electoral relevance. Fortunately, I thought at the time, and for some time afterwards, such thinking has had its day. But I was wrong.

Analogous to an Economic Groundhog Day, our polity continues to relive the economic debate of the early 1980s, which hung on the question: Is a tightly regulated, high tax, nationalised economy better for society than a deregulated, low tax, privatised one? Many of us thought, naively it turns out, that question was answered a generation ago with a resounding, No. With the advantage of hindsight, however, it is clear that we were correct only in an empirical sense. In the political world, the economic flat-earthers never went away; they merely faded into the policy background to await their next moment in the fiscal sun, which arrived in 2008 in the form of a global recession. And, over the past two years, how the Wilkinsons and Picketts of this world have enjoyed their intellectually lazy, empirically hazy days of summer.

Hence, the need for an intellectual push-back the likes of which Christopher Snowdon so comprehensively provides in this volume. Most impressively, perhaps, Snowdon's refutation of Wilkinson, Pickett *et al.* is both measured and finely balanced. When confronted with arguments and 'facts' that constitute little more than 'junk economics', it is very tempting, although rarely advantageous, to focus upon either the ignorance or the ineptitude of the researcher(s) in question. To his considerable credit, Snowdon resists the temptation to match his opponents' tactics.

In striking contrast to so much contemporary anti-capitalist rhetoric, Snowdon's words are calm, considered, and constructive. He simply lets his impressive empiricism do the talking for him. Having marshalled an immense body of evidence, he needs neither overheated language nor overblown conclusions.

Snowdon's serious and careful treatment of his subject illustrates what, on our better days, we hope the Democracy Institute is all about. His ability to find the methodological flaws within specific pieces of research, unearth and explain contrasting pieces of research, and present this set of conclusions in an accessible manner is a skill possessed by a comparative few and one for which his readers should be thankful.

I am especially thankful for the realisation that, although I am an alleged expert in several of the specific areas covered in his book, I learned a considerable number of interesting things while reading it. I strongly suspect that everyone who reads this book will experience similar growth.

Patrick Basham

Democracy Institute

London

April 2010

Introduction

In March 2009, a book was published which promised to revolutionise the way we look at the world. Written by two British epidemiologists—Richard Wilkinson and Kate Pickett— *The Spirit Level: Why more equal societies almost always do better* argued that developed societies had reached the limit of what could be achieved from economic growth. Evidence from around the world showed that people in rich countries no longer benefited from higher incomes. Despite their wealth, they were not getting healthier or happier, rather they were experiencing a worsening of social problems.

Through a scientific analysis of the world's richest countries, Wilkinson and Pickett claimed to have found a remarkable pattern. Every major health and social problem that afflicted society was directly linked to levels of income inequality. Countries with a wide gap between rich and poor had lower life expectancies, higher rates of infant mortality, lower standards of education and higher murder rates. The people who lived in them were five times more likely to be in jail, five times more likely to be mentally ill, six times more likely to be obese and many times more likely to be murdered.

It was an astonishing claim. If true, it was the kind of grand unifying theory that comes along once in a generation. Its implications for politicians were obvious: instead of chasing economic growth which will only make us sicker, they must divert their efforts towards redistributing wealth. Sweden and Denmark had it right. Britain and the USA had it wrong.

But they went further. It had long been recognised that poor health, violence and low educational achievement were more common amongst the poor. It had also long been recognised that economic growth benefited the poor by lifting overall living standards, creating jobs and improving public services. Since capitalism had been shown to be the most effective system for generating growth, it was, *QED*, the best system for society as a whole. Higher taxes and wealth redistribution would slow growth and should be opposed.

Wilkinson and Pickett argued that this was no longer the case. Unequal societies did badly not because more people were poor—absolute poverty had been practically eradicated in all the countries they studied—but because inequality acted like a virus. It was how much money *other* people had that caused the problem. Inequality wreaked psychological damage: people were less trusting, less community-minded, more greedy and more insecure in less equal countries. This damage could not be undone by making everyone wealthier; it could only be undone by narrowing the gap between rich and poor.

As portrayed in *The Spirit Level*, life in countries such as Britain and the USA is a soul-destroying rat race filled with anxious, unhappy individuals who, when not working long hours in meaningless jobs, spend their lives buying products they neither need nor truly want.

The minds of the less wealthy are crippled by the memory of shattered dreams and their failure to keep pace with the David Beckhams and Paris Hiltons. They are the losers, the outsiders, destined never to possess the status symbols they see relentlessly advertised on television. Broken mentally, they suffer panic attacks and depression before descending into a spiral of drug use and violence.

Life for the rich in unequal countries is scarcely any better. The most affluent members of society lead vacuous lives of rampant consumerism. Nervously looking over their shoulder at the person who might take their job, or jealously peering over their neighbour's fence, they can never be satisfied. The pursuit of ever greater riches cannot fill the existential void. Constantly anxious about their status, and living in a society of private opulence and public squalour, they become depressed, alienated, unwell, violent and, in some instances, homicidal.

Regardless of wealth, then, living in an unequal society was harmful to all. Unequal societies bred mental illness and poor health amongst rich and poor alike. Everyone, therefore, stood to gain from greater equality.

Rapturously received by much of the media, *The Spirit Level* became one of the publishing sensations of the year. Here, it seemed, was the long-awaited scientific proof that higher taxes and wealth redistribution really do create the happiest, healthiest and most peaceful societies. *The Guardian*'s Polly Toynbee described it as "groundbreaking research"[1] and called lead author Richard Wilkinson "a kind of Darwin figure."[2] Toynbee's colleague Lynsey Hanley saluted *The Spirit Level*'s "inarguable battery of evidence."[3] Ken Livingstone applauded it for providing "proof that most of the ills of our 'broken society' arise out of the growing inequality of the past 30 years."[4]

Several reviewers commended *The Spirit Level* for providing the evidence to back up what every decent person had always believed to be true. It provided a rational foundation for intuitive passions. Yasmin Alibhai-Brown wrote in *The Independent*:

As a social democrat perhaps I am viscerally (and irrationally) repulsed by the super-affluent and their show-off lifestyles. But others have looked at their effect coolly, and tested the model. What they find is worse than anyone could have predicted. The most recent study is the most compelling and shocking. All free marketeers should be made to memorise it from cover to cover.[5]

The Sunday Times said the book "formulates what everyone has always felt" and "turns personal intuitions into publicly demonstrable facts."[6] Reviewing it in the *New Statesman*, Roy Hattersley said it "demonstrates the scientific truth of the assertion that social democrats have made for a hundred years—sometimes more out of hope than intellectual certainty."[7]

By the end of 2009, both Hattersley and Livingstone had named it as their book of the year and the *New Statesman* named it as one of the top ten books of the decade. When it was published in paperback the following March, its subtitle was changed from 'Why more equal societies almost always do better' to the less equivocal 'Why equality is better for everyone.'[8]

By January 2010, just 9 months after publication, *The Spirit Level* was being cited in the House of Lords. Under discussion was the government's Equality Bill, the speaker was Baroness Royal:

"A number of noble Lords referred on Second Reading to the work of the Equality Trust, which was summarised in a book, *The Spirit Level*, much quoted in this Chamber. The gist of the authors' impressive research is that societies that are more equal in terms of income distribution tend to be better societies in every way — richer, healthier, happier, more cohesive, less prone to violent crime and so on. I concur with that analysis, which is why we need the socio-economic duty."[9]

The Spirit Level offered a whole new way of looking at politics. Almost by accident, it seemed, two sober and disinterested scientists had proven beyond reasonable doubt that narrowing the wealth gap and restricting economic growth was the panacea for all social ills. The implications could scarcely be exaggerated and its authors had no intention of playing them down. Comparing their findings to those of Louis Pasteur and Joseph Lister, they wrote: "Understanding the effects of inequality means that we suddenly have a policy handle on the wellbeing of whole societies."[10]

There was just one problem. In political terms it was not a huge problem. Greater obstacles had been overcome in the past and yet, for sticklers and pedants, it remained a problem.

It wasn't true.

Methodology

The authors of *The Spirit Level* chose which countries to study by looking at the world's 50 richest nations and selecting the most suitable. Countries such as Iceland, which have no reliable data on inequality, were understandably left out. They also excluded all nations with populations of under 3 million on the basis that they did not want to include tax havens.

Ignoring tax havens makes perfect sense, but that could have been achieved by simply excluding known tax havens. The 3 million cut-off point seems arbitrary and only serves to exclude Slovenia from the analysis. Slovenia is the world's 46th richest country,[1] has a population of over 2 million and is by no means a tax haven. In some of their earlier studies, Wilkinson and Pickett included Slovenia in their analysis, but dropped it for *The Spirit Level*.[2] For this analysis, Slovenia has been reinstated.

There are several other notable absentees from Wilkinson and Pickett's list. The inclusion of Japan provided them with an example of a successful country with a narrow gap between rich and poor. But while they include Japan, the equally successful—but far less equal—Singapore only gets occasional mentions. Wilkinson and Pickett explain that they could not find relevant data, but rates of, for example, obesity and mental illness are readily available and have been included in this analysis.

More puzzlingly, the Republic of Korea and Hong Kong were left out entirely, despite their wealth. Both of these nations are examined in this book and, by doing so, we are better able to judge whether Japan benefits from low inequality or whether other, less equal Asian countries see the same benefits. Singapore and Hong Kong's inclusion is particularly useful since they are at the opposite end of the equality scale to Japan, less equal than even the USA.

In *The Spirit Level*, Portugal generally performs quite poorly, which the authors attribute to its high level of inequality. It is, however, by far the poorest country in their analysis, with a per capita Gross National Income (GNI) $3,000 lower than the next poorest country, Greece. To test whether Portugal is suffering from a lack of equality or a lack of wealth, the Czech Republic and Hungary have been included here.

The Czech Republic is actually wealthier than Portugal (as shown on page 7 of *The Spirit Level*) and its absence from Wilinson and Pickett's study is hard to explain.[3] Hungary is somewhat poorer, with a per capita GNI $3,000 lower than Portugal. Hungary therefore plays a similar role in this book to that which Portugal played in *The Spirit Level*. Hungary may perform badly because of its relative lack of wealth or it may perform well as a result of its low level of inequality. Hungary, Slovenia and the Czech Republic all have a narrow gap between rich and poor, making them ideal case studies against which to compare unequal Portugal.

By expanding the analysis to include several other comparable countries, it not only gives the inequality hypothesis an opportunity to prove itself over a broader spectrum, it also allows us to compare like with like. With the exception of Hungary, all these countries are wealthier than Portugal, and all are classified by the United Nations as being of 'high human development.'[4]

The measure of inequality used in this book is identical to that used in *The Spirit Level*. It is the gap between the richest and poorest 20% of the population, eg. the richest 20% in Spain have an average income that is 5.5 times higher than the average income of the bottom 20%. The same UN source has been used to calculate this.[5]

Most graphs are shown with a linear regression line. As in *The Spirit Level*, these lines are dictated by a standard computer program which finds the best fit from the data provided. In addition, each graph shows the value of the square of the correlation coefficient (R^2). This gives a value for the best fit, ranging from 0 (no correlation) to 1 (perfect correlation). Although this allows comparisons to be made between different data sets, readers are urged to use their own judgement when interpreting scatter graphs. As we shall see, comparing statistics from whole nations is far from being a perfect science. Correlation does not necessarily equal causation and one or two outliers can give the appearance of a trend which may not be supported by the rest of the data.

Unless otherwise noted, the same sources have been used for the various health and social problems studied. Since some of the figures used in *The Spirit Level* differ from those shown here, detailed notes and references can be found at the back of this book, along with website addresses for all the main United Nations, World Bank, Organisation for Economic Co-operation and Development (OECD) and World Values Survey data, where these facts can be easily verified*. A healthy scepticism is encouraged at all times.

---

* This book will discuss international comparisons, which form the main body of *The Spirit Level*. Wilkinson and Pickett use comparisons between US states as supporting evidence but since the 'least equal' states are also the poorest and most ethnically diverse states, it is impossible to distinguish the effects of inequality from other socio-economic factors. A fuller discussion of this issue can be read at www.spiritleveldelusion.com.

Methodology

1

Bad for our health?

"Average life expectancy is three or four years shorter in unequal societies"
— claim made in *The Spirit Level* (p. 84)

In May 2001, a remarkable study appeared in *Annals of Internal Medicine* which seemed to demonstrate that the psychological trauma of failure leads to poor health and premature death. Two researchers studied the longevity of Hollywood actors and found that Oscar winners lived, on average, four years longer than those who had been nominated and lost, as well as those who had never been nominated at all. Those who won multiple Oscars lived no fewer than six years longer. This difference in life expectancy was, as the researchers concluded with no little hyperbole, "about equal to the societal consequences of curing all cancers in all people for all time."[1]

It was an eye-catching finding, and not just because it involved movie stars. It seemed to offer solid proof that success and status have a significant impact on physical health. It showed that the health and longevity of even the richest and most successful people are largely determined by where they stand amongst their peers.

This idea is central to *The Spirit Level*'s hypothesis that inequality leads to poor health and, therefore, reduced life expectancy. This controversial theory can be traced back to January 1992 when the *British Medical Journal (BMJ)* published an article titled 'Income distribution and life expectancy' which showed higher life expectancies in countries where the poorest 70% of families received a larger proportion of national income. At the bottom of the scale was West Germany, where life expectancy was just over 73 years. At the top of the pile sat Sweden and Norway, with life expectancies of around 76 years.

The study concluded that if Britain adopted "an income distribution more like the most egalitarian European countries" it would increase average life spans by two years.[2] The author of the study was Richard Wilkinson, an epidemiologist who had been banging the drum of inequality for some time. Studying at Nottingham University in 1976, Wilkinson's Masters thesis was titled 'Socio-economic factors in mortality differentials'. In the same year, he wrote an open letter to the Secretary of State for Social Services, David Ennals, in the left-wing magazine *New Society*.[3]

Wilkinson's letter called for an urgent enquiry into health inequalities and led directly to the Labour government commissioning *Inequalities in Health*. Better known as the Black Report, after its chairman Sir Douglas Black, this document was finally published in 1980 under a Conservative administration which released it on a bank holiday to guarantee minimum publicity. The Conservatives' distain for the report can be explained by the fact that, as the Socialist Health Association put it: "Redistribution, increased public expenditure and taxation and unashamed socialism are flaunted on almost every page."[4]

Throughout the 1980s, Wilkinson continued his research into the relationship between income inequality and health. In 1991, the Socialist Health Association published his book *Towards Equality in Health: Income and Health* in which he asserted that "economic growth no longer ensures rising standards of health."[5] Not for the last time, Wilkinson used international comparisons of life expectancy to support his claim that standards of health in developed countries were primarily dictated by levels of inequality.

Towards Equality in Health was followed by *Unhealthy Societies: The Affliction of Inequality* (1996) and *The Impact of Inequality: How to Make Sick Societies Healthier* (2006). Despite the Damascene conversion portrayed in *The Spirit Level*, Wilkinson had made up his mind that inequality was the key to health and well-being at least two decades before that book was published.

Wilkinson's 1992 article in the *British Medical Journal* inspired a flurry of research, and in *The Spirit Level*, the authors refer to a "vast literature" on the subject. There is, however, no mention of how much of this vast literature was written by Wilkinson himself, nor that much of the rest was critical of his theory.

His *BMJ* study was debunked at length in the same journal in 1995 by Ken Judge.[6] Judge pointed out numerous errors in Wilkinson's research, including the use of "inappropriate" data. He criticised Wilkinson for using the lowest 70% of families as a measure of inequality when a more conventional measure is the bottom 10% or 20% of individuals. "The suspicion," wrote Judge, "must be that the choice is derived from the data" (ie. Wilkinson was cherry-picking). When Judge recalculated the data based on the more usual measure of income per head, the association between life expectancy and inequality disappeared.

Judge concluded:

In retrospect, it seems extraordinary that a predominantly monocausal explanation of international variations in life expectancy should ever have been regarded as plausible. It is much more likely that they are the product of many influences, which probably interact over long periods of time.

Further studies conducted in Denmark[7] and Japan[8] failed to support Wilkinson's hypothesis and although some studies showed an association between income inequality and life expectancy in the USA, other evidence showed that this was more likely to be due to education[9], underinvestment[10] and other confounding factors.[11] In 2002, a large study of wealthy European countries showed no association between inequality and life expectancy.[12]

As the case for the inequality hypothesis broke down, so too did the related claim (also made by Wilkinson) that life expectancy was not related to economic growth. Using figures from 1975-85, Wilkinson had claimed that once average income exceeded $5,000 a year, further wealth no longer drove up life expectancy (nb. $5,000 in 1984 is the equivalent of $10,500 today). There was, he explained, no point chasing economic growth beyond that level:

In 1984 few countries achieved an average life expectancy at birth of 70 years or more until gross national product per head approached a threshold of $5000 a year. Beyond that level it seems that there is little systematic relation between gross national product per head and life expectancy.[13]

However, as was soon noticed, Wilkinson had been rather selective in picking which countries to study, excluding ten of the 33 countries which had a per capita GDP of over $10,000. When a team of epidemiologists redrew the graph with all 33 countries included, a positive correlation between average income and life expectancy became apparent. People in the richest countries did indeed live longest. Couching their criticism of Wilkinson in the most delicate terms, they wrote that "the strength of the association between absolute income and life expectancy seems quite sensitive to which countries are included."[14] In layman's terms, Wilkinson had been cherry-picking his data again.

In *The Spirit Level*, Wilkinson and Pickett cite a 1996 editorial from the *BMJ* which discussed the "big idea" that "the more equally wealth is distributed the better the health of that society."[15] At that time, the *BMJ* was broadly supportive of the theory but research into it was still in its infancy. Wilkinson and

Pickett do not mention the editorial that appeared in the same journal six years later, which concluded:

Now that good data on income inequality have become available for 16 western industrialised countries, the association between income inequality and life expectancy has disappeared.[16]

The inequality-life expectancy hypothesis may have been losing credibility, but the link between low income and low life expectancy remained strong. Poor housing, an unhealthy diet, urban pollution, long working hours and the other trappings of poverty made such an association likely and, more importantly, it was supported by the data. It was also conceivable, if largely theoretical, that being wealthy could result in poor health if it led to a sedentary lifestyle and the over-consumption of alcohol, tobacco and fatty foods.

But whilst there were plausible biological reasons why income might affect health, it was harder to explain how inequality could, in itself, create health problems. How could it be healthier to earn £10,000 in a country where that was the average wage than to earn £12,000 in a country where £20,000 was the average wage? This was the critical question that Wilkinson needed to answer and he did so by advancing the theory of "psychosocial pathways".

Relative inequality, he said, led to isolation, insecurity, anxiety, low self-esteem, chronic stress and depression. He found support from Dr Michael Marmot, an epidemiologist who had found differences in life expectancy amongst the British civil service, with those at the top of the hierarchy living longest and those at the bottom dying soonest. Together, they made the case that there were fewer social networks in unequal countries and that the resulting stress led to early graves.

Marmot outlined this theory in his 2004 book *Status Syndrome* and Wilkinson reiterates it in *The Spirit Level*, along with the assertion that fewer people are members of community organisations in less equal countries. As we shall see in Chapter

3, this last claim is untrue. Indeed, Dr John Lynch and his colleagues found the reverse to be the case. In their study of 15 wealthy countries, they found that:

Indicators of social capital, such as trust and belonging to and volunteering for community organisations, were all much more strongly related to gross domestic product than to income inequality.[17]

Nevertheless, Wilkinson maintained that inequality "gets under the skin" to produce psychological ailments which manifest themselves in physical illnesses such as coronary heart disease. This, of course, was hard to prove, although there is some evidence that one's state of mind can affects one's health. Stress, for example, is a risk factor for stomach ulcers and the phenomenon of the recently widowed 'dying of a broken heart' is not without empirical evidence.[18]

But even if status envy was a risk factor for ill-health—and this was far from proven—its impact could not possibly be seen in the overall life expectancy of a nation. Smoking, for instance, is a very significant risk factor for a number of fatal diseases and yet it is impossible to tell from international comparisons of life expectancy which countries have high rates of smoking. Even major risk factors become submerged in the mass of data.

If anything, the international data contradicted Wilkinson's hypothesis. It was difficult to tally the dramatic decline in heart disease in the late twentieth century with rising levels of inequality. Noting the "impressive declines in mortality, especially from cardiovascular causes" in Finland, Britain, Japan, New Zealand and the USA, Dr Lynch drily commented that "it is not likely that these are the results of improved interpersonal networks and social support."[19]

More plausible, at least superficially, was the theory of 'psychosocial' pressures leading people to indulge in unhealthy pursuits such as excessive eating, drinking and smoking. These were all widely regarded as risk factors for poor health and an early death. If they were more common in unequal societies, it would be reasonable to expect lower life expectancies.

In fact, there is no relationship between inequality and obesity and there is, if anything, an inverse relationship between inequality and both smoking and alcohol consumption.

Cigarettes and alcohol

Figure 1.1 shows per capita alcohol consumption in 2003, the last year for which full records are available.[20] There is a modest trend towards people in more equal countries consuming more alcohol, largely as a result of the Czech Republic's high intake and Singapore's low intake. Certainly, there is no evidence of the reverse being the case.

People in Sweden and Norway appear to consume relatively little alcohol, but the higher consumption of the Finns, Danes, Hungarians and Czechs suggests that this is very unlikely to be related to their more egalitarian economic systems. It is far more likely to be the result of the exceptionally high price of alcohol in Sweden and Norway. According to a European Commission report, Norway has "probably had the most restrictive alcohol

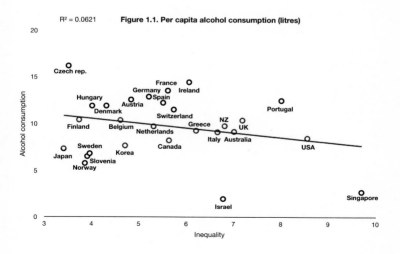

$R^2 = 0.0621$ **Figure 1.1. Per capita alcohol consumption (litres)**

23

policy in Europe" while Sweden has the highest alcohol taxes in the EU.[21] Sweden's alcohol retail industry (*Systembolaget*) is a government monopoly which only sells to those over the age of 20. Norway and Finland have similar state-run organisations for the sale of hard liquor.

Because of the high tax rate, cross-border trafficking is widespread, particularly to Denmark, whose much higher rate of consumption partly reflects sales to its Nordic neighbours. The Danes, in turn, buy a great deal of their alcohol from Germany. And because this graph only shows recorded alcohol sales, Scandinavia's extensive home-brewing industry—another side effect of temperance controls—is not reflected at all.

Far from being a tribute to Scandinavian socialism, then, the lower rates of alcohol consumption in Sweden and Norway are a reflection of the paternalistic and authoritarian alcohol policies of their governments.

Figure 1.2 shows smoking prevalence for males over 14 years old. Females have been excluded because smoking remains at least partially taboo for women in several countries. The data are taken from 2001-04 except when unavailable.[22] Korea is a

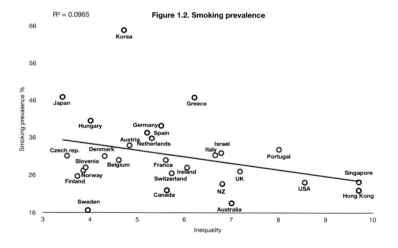

Figure 1.2. Smoking prevalence

huge outlier with male smoking prevalence of 64.9% but the inverse correlation remains even if it is excluded.

Contrary to Wilkinson's hypothesis, there is evidence of smoking being less common in unequal societies. The association is quite strong, although it may be due to persistent tobacco control policies in the USA, Australia, Singapore and Hong Kong. Whatever the cause, there is no evidence that the supposed psychosocial pressures of life in the less equal countries have led to higher smoking rates.

Obesity

Nor is there evidence that the other much-discussed risk factor for an early death—obesity—is more common in unequal societies. Statistics for obesity prevalence are not especially reliable and international data collection is sporadic at best. Wilkinson and Pickett use data from the International Obesity Task Force (IOTF), a campaigning organisation whose mission is to "inform the world about the urgency of the problem and to persuade governments that the time to act is now."[23] The IOTF does not have the resources to collect its own data and instead relies on individual epidemiological studies carried out by different researchers, using different methodologies over a period of many years. They are by no means definitive.

The figure the IOTF currently uses for Sweden, for example, is based on data from just one city.[24] Greece's peculiarly high obesity rate of nearly 30% shown in *The Spirit Level* was based on a limited age-group. The IOTF has since abandoned that figure in favour of 17.5%, as reported in a subsequent larger study.[25] This gives an indication of how much statistics can fluctuate depending on study design.

One problem is that, since no government is yet prepared to weigh and measure all its citizens, all these studies rely on samples ranging from a few hundred to a few thousand people. Many of them rely on individuals reporting their own weight, a highly unsatisfactory method since it is well-established that many people, particularly women and the obese, tend to under-report this.[26]

A further limitation is the time gap between surveys. It is well-known that obesity prevalence has risen significantly in the last twenty years in most Western countries. Unfortunately, while we have recent data for countries like the USA and Britain, the most recent figures for places like Belgium and Hungary date from the early and mid-1990s. As such, they almost certainly under-represent the true scale of obesity today.

Nevertheless, some data is (probably) better than no data at all and figure 1.3 shows the IOTF's best estimates for obesity prevalence between 1994 and 2004.[27] Apart from the correction of the Greek anomaly, and the addition of countries such as Singapore and Israel, which were excluded from Wilkinson and Pickett's analysis, most of the data is identical to that shown in *The Spirit Level*.[28]

Once the missing countries are added, the tenuous correlation between obesity and inequality disappears altogether. Although Wilkinson and Pickett put an upward line through

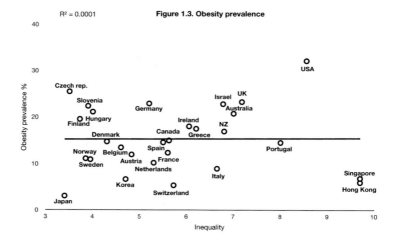

Figure 1.3. Obesity prevalence

their graph, this is only possible thanks to the erroneous Greek figure, the exclusion of Singapore and the fact that the USA and Japan are obvious outliers.[29]

The positions of Singapore, Korea and Hong Kong in figure 1.3 strongly suggest that Japan's relative skinniness is related to the Asian diet and/or genetics rather than the gap between rich and poor. The failure of Wilkinson and Pickett to show any Asian country other than Japan in their graph restricts their analysis and produces a misleading picture.

Life expectancy

The final, and most powerful, piece of evidence regarding health and inequality comes from the life expectancy figures themselves. Wilkinson and Pickett present a graph in *The Spirit Level* showing life expectancy against inequality. This is recreated in figure 1.4 and is based on data from the 2004 United Nations Human Development Report.[30] There does indeed seem to be a downward trend as countries become less equal, largely as a

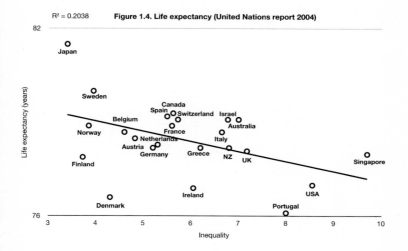

Figure 1.4. Life expectancy (United Nations report 2004)

result of Japan and Sweden's high standing and Portugal and the USA's poor position.

There is, however, something odd about their choice of source material for this graph. Why have they used the 2004 report when the 2005 and 2006 reports were available to them? They rely on the 2006 report extensively elsewhere in the book, and even use its life expectancy figures in another graph, so why use older data here?[31]

That question is answered by figure 1.5, which shows life expectancy as presented in the 2006 report.[32] The correlation has gone, replaced by a modest trend in the opposite direction. In the space of just two years, Sweden has been overtaken by several less equal countries. The presence of Hong Kong shows that very unequal countries can have long life expectancies, while egalitarian Denmark and Korea perform poorly. By showing missing countries like Slovenia and the Czech Republic, we can see that Portugal's low standing is likely due to it being relatively less wealthy. As its economy grows, so too does its life expectancy.

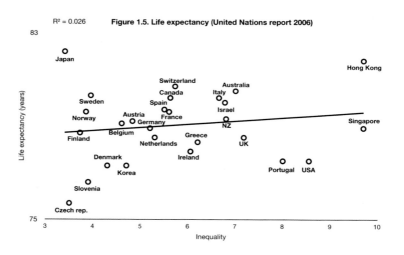

Figure 1.5. Life expectancy (United Nations report 2006)

It seems that Wilkinson and Pickett picked a moment in time during which there was a rough correlation that suited their hypothesis. The inequality-life expectancy hypothesis is not only "quite sensitive to which countries are included", but also quite sensitive to which years are examined. A scientific law that only works in certain circumstances at certain times is, of course, no law at all.

To demonstrate that the life expectancy figures in the 2006 UN Report were not anomalous, figure 1.6 presents the evidence from the 2009 UN Report, which confirms that life expectancy is not linked to inequality*.[33]

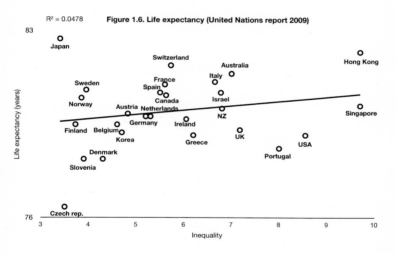

Figure 1.6. Life expectancy (United Nations report 2009)

The 2009 report had not been published when *The Spirit Level* was being written, but every pillar of Wilkinson's inequality hypothesis had been tested and found wanting long before then. There was scant evidence that unequal societies inflicted psychosocial pressures on their people to a greater extent than

* In 2010, Kate Pickett produced a video titled 'Why Cubans Live Longer Than Americans'. In fact, life expectancy is higher in the USA (79.1 years) than in Cuba (78.5 years).[34]

was the case in more egalitarian nations. Neither heart disease nor overall mortality rose in countries which became significantly less equal after the 1970s. Life expectancy rose at a similar rate in virtually all developed countries and continues to do so. Without some dramatic breakthrough, such as a cure for cancer, future rises in life expectancy in developed countries will be far more sluggish than those seen in the twentieth century. This is only to be expected as we draw closer to the biological limits of longevity.

No one doubted that poverty was a risk factor for ill-health even in wealthy societies, nor did anyone dispute the need for improving health-care and facilities for all. The question was whether the free market was better able to raise overall standards than central planning. By the 1990s, those who preferred the latter were a dwindling minority due, in no small part, to the bankruptcy of the Soviet Union and its satellite states.

Wilkinson's life expectancy hypothesis was a novel way of reinvigorating the left by creating a health issue which, by definition, could only be solved by reducing inequality through wealth redistribution and higher taxation. It had obvious appeal to people far beyond the circle of epidemiologists who would normally concern themselves with such theories. Within three years of Wilkinson's 1992 study being published, it had been cited in over 30 articles in 16 different journals, and its findings had been used by the World Bank, World Health Organisation and the Commission on Social Justice.

Despite this publicity, Wilkinson's theory was undone by the facts. Having studied the figures from 1975-85, he believed the mid-1980s represented the end of an era, and that rising prosperity would never again lead to further rises in life expectancy. But, rather inconveniently, life expectancy *did* continue to rise in line with national income and more equal countries conspicuously failed to fare any better than the rest.

Between 1981 and 2007, life expectancy in Britain rose from 74 years to 79.3 years. Sweden's life expectancy also rose—

to 80.8 years—but less equal countries such as Italy and Australia saw still higher life expectancies (81.1 and 81.4 years respectively). In the same period, egalitarian Denmark dropped to the bottom of the list, overtaken by every single country studied in *The Spirit Level*.[35]

By the time *The Spirit Level* was published, the slender circumstantial evidence upon which Wilkinson had made his case had been obliterated with the passing of time. Rather than change the theory to fit the facts, he and Pickett ignored the facts and persisted with the theory. In practice, that meant using obsolete data when they were quite aware that more recent data was available.

Messing with our minds

2

Messing with our minds

"Rates of mental illness are five times higher in the most unequal
countries compared to the least unequal countries"
— back cover of *The Spirit Level*

If inequality does not make us physically unwell, perhaps it does, at least, make us mentally unwell. This is the second argument put forward in *The Spirit Level*.

Wilkinson and Pickett argue that an unequal distribution of wealth creates an environment in which emotional distress and mental disorders flourish. The rich and poor are equally susceptible. The wealthy man on his perpetual hamster-wheel tries to keep up with the Joneses in a way that can never satisfy his innate emotional needs. The poor man wallows at the bottom, watching advertisements for products he will never possess while never appreciating what he already has. Consequently, depression and anxiety are far more common in unequal societies.

This theory was popularised by the psychologist Oliver James in his 2007 book *Affluenza*. In it, James describes what he calls Selfish Capitalism as a virus spreading across the English-speaking world. Selfish Capitalism, he argues, was spawned by the free market economics of Thatcher and Reagan which valued material possessions above 'authentic' life and kept people in a spiral of gruelling work and consumerism. This economic system, James argued, breeds a preoccupation with money, possessions, fame and appearance; what he calls 'Virus values'. America is the worst infected country, he says, Denmark the least.

Oliver was by no means the first person to make such a critique of modern life. Michael Marmot had covered similar ground in *Status Syndrome* (2004), and James' one-time colleague Richard Layard had done likewise in *Happiness: Lessons from a New Science* (2005). Even the term 'Affluenza' was borrowed from a 2002 book titled *Affluenza: The All-Consuming Epidemic* which had a similar anti-consumerist theme.

Although he and Layard had been part of the 'happiness forum' that advised Tony Blair's government, James was dismissive about the very concept of happiness. In his view, consumer capitalism had more to answer for than making people feel glum. Unless vigorously curtailed by the state, he saw it leading to clinical depression, anxiety disorders and many other neuroses, as he explained in a radio interview:

"I don't hold with all this happiness stuff. I don't think we can be happy. Don't be so silly. What do you mean? Happiness is an ephemeral state that I get from smoking a cigarette or having sex. It passes very quickly. That's not what I'm talking about. I'm talking about *mental health*. I'm talking about trying to create forms of political governance which provide a framework for the population to be mentally healthy."[1]

The virus of Affluenza, then, was stalking the globe. It began in the English-speaking nations which had been first to adopt free market economics, and was now travelling further afield. James' evidence for all this was a curious mix of autobiography and anecdote. *Affluenza* sees the consumerism-hating psychologist jetting around the world interviewing middle-aged millionaires and catching up with old chums from Eton and Cambridge. Although he tells his readers that they don't need to buy frivolous items such as DVD players ("you have already got a video"), James purchases a portable DVD player before he sets off in order "to keep our [twenty-one month old] daughter quiet."[2]

The round-the-world trip that follows only reinforces James' belief that the Virus is spreading. Those who complain about life's trials and tribulations are diagnosed as mentally unwell. Those who declare themselves happy are said to be in denial. With the exception of a Nigerian taxi-driver who seems cheerful enough, James does not encounter anyone lower down the socio-economic ladder who might exhibit the same stress and *ennui* as the Selfish Capitalists who dominate his research.

It is little wonder that James diagnosed Affluenza wherever he turned, as the symptoms are remarkably broad. Tell-tale signs include a desire to "successfully hide the signs of ageing" and to "keep up with fashions in hair and clothing", two ambitions that would put most women, and many men, in the 'infected' camp. Other statements that show a person has contracted the Virus include: "My life would be better if I owned certain things I don't have now" and "I would like to be admired by many people."[3]

Anecdotal evidence aside, James' proof that mental illness was linked to Selfish Capitalism relied on the *post hoc ergo propter hoc* observation that the rise in recorded emotional distress in English-speaking countries began around 1980, just as neoconservatism was taking hold. In the follow up to *Affluenza—The Selfish Capitalist—*James sets out his position in no uncertain terms:

To be absolutely clear, my new assertions are that

Selfish Capitalism led to a massive increase in the wealth of the wealthy, with no rise in average wages

and

there has been a substantial increase in emotional distress since the 1970s
(Italics in the original)[4]

The first assertion is simply wrong. The rich may have got richer in the last thirty years, but wages have increased universally. This is true of all classes, in all Western countries and remains true whether you measure wages by the hour, week or year. According to the Trade Union Congress—not an organisation disposed to neoconservatism—the average wage in Britain, adjusted for inflation, rose by 56% between 1978 and 2008.[5] In the USA, estimates for the rise in real median earnings between 1979 and 2003 vary from 10.5% to 32.2%. It is true that in both countries, the lowest earners saw their wages rise more slowly than those on the highest incomes. It is also true that wages have not always risen in line with gross national income. But it is undeniable that there *was* a rise.

The second of James' assertions is the subject of this chapter, since it forms the basis of *The Spirit Level*'s claim that people living in unequal countries are five times more likely to suffer from mental illness than those in the most equal countries. To provide support for this theory in *Affluenza*, James turned to Richard Wilkinson and Kate Pickett.

The two epidemiologists created a graph that would appear two years later, in augmented form, in *The Spirit Level*. It showed, in percentage terms, how many people had suffered a mental disorder in the past 12 months. They had first used the graph in a preliminary study published in an epidemiological journal in 2006.[6] It was not, in all honesty, particularly compelling. Based on a World Health Organisation (WHO) survey, it showed just eight countries, five of which had low rates of mental distress, despite a wide variation in inequality (Japan, Germany, Belgium, Spain and Italy). France and the Netherlands were a little higher up the graph and the USA was significantly higher.

For publication in *Affluenza*, Wilkinson and Pickett dug out figures for New Zealand, Singapore, Canada, Britain and Australia from other sources and added them to the graph.[7] These figures were also high, though not quite as high as

America's, and a trend was now taking shape. James had found his smoking gun: mental illness was more common in English-speaking countries. He published the graph in both *Affluenza* and *The Selfish Capitalist* and began spreading the word to anyone who would listen, as in this interview:

"One of the most extraordinary statistics that I've discovered through my research is that in the English-speaking world, where we have Selfish Capitalist political governance and where the Affluenza virus is rife, we also have *twice as much* mental illness. That's an incredible fact. I can't understand why that hasn't been a news story everywhere in the UK... Don't ever listen to anyone who tells you it's all about genes. This is sure evidence that it's not."[8]

The data James relied upon is shown in figure 2.1. Since this graph has been reproduced so often and is so crucial to the ideas expressed in both *Affluenza* and *The Spirit Level*, we might take a moment to test its veracity.

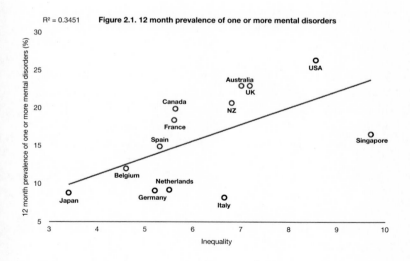

$R^2 = 0.3451$ **Figure 2.1. 12 month prevalence of one or more mental disorders**

(Singapore is shown in *Affluenza* but not in *The Spirit Level*.
The Canadian study is actually a study of the population of Ontario only.)

Mixing and matching

Gauging rates of mental illness is hampered by the failure of many countries to collect or publish reliable data. Only a handful of nations—notably Germany and the USA—produce useable data and at least a dozen EU countries, including Portugal, Ireland and Greece, produce nothing at all.[9]

Wilkinson and Pickett used figures from various different sources to compile their graph of 'mental illness' (this term and 'emotional distress' are interchangeable). They admitted that these statistics were "not strictly comparable" but this only hints at the underlying problem with this mix and match approach.

The figures for all the European countries, apart from the UK, came from a 2004 study from the World Mental Health Survey Consortium (WMH)*.[10] Wilkinson and Pickett portray the WMH, set up by the World Health Organisation, as being near-definitive. They do not mention another WHO project called the International Consortium in Psychiatric Epidemiology (ICPE)[11] which came up with very different figures a year earlier. The full WMH and ICPE results are shown in figures 2.2 and 2.3.

Note the large disparity between the estimates for Germany and the Netherlands. According to the ICPE, prevalence of mental disorders in the Netherlands is 23.3%, considerably higher than the 14.9% recorded by the WMH.[12] The WMH's figure for Germany (9.1%) is dramatically lower than the ICPE's figure of 24% and, tellingly, also lower than the 31% reported in the German Health Interview and Examination Survey.[13]

The EU average for mental disorder prevalence, based on evidence from 27 studies and 16 countries, is 27%.[14] Studies of Western European nations have found rates of mental disorder in the range of 20-40%. In the WMH study, however, the range is half of that: 8-19%. In short, the WMH study appears to

* All figures below, as in *The Spirit Level*, refer to adults' experience of mental disorder in the last 12 months.

underestimate the prevalence of mental disorders in Europe. It is inconsistent with nationwide studies produced at around the same time and with the ICPE survey.

For some reason, technical or methodological, the study upon which Wilkinson, Pickett and James hang their entire case

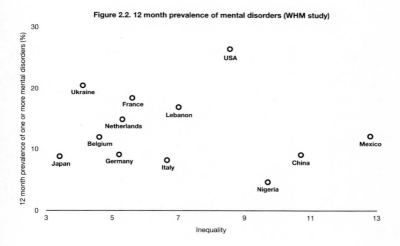

Figure 2.2. 12 month prevalence of mental disorders (WHM study)

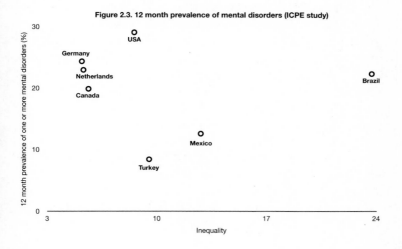

Figure 2.3. 12 month prevalence of mental disorders (ICPE study)

downplays the scale of mental disorder in European countries. A reading of the study's text reveals that there were indeed technical problems relating to the European data.

A related limitation is that the Western European surveys, which were fielded before any of the other WMH surveys, experienced a number of difficulties in survey implementation, largely skip logic errors, that subsequently surveys avoided because they were resolved while carrying out the Western European surveys. As a result, these early surveys had much more item-missing data than later surveys, which led to underestimation of severity of some disorders.[15]

Furthermore, the authors admit that "various of the WMH surveys deleted disorders that were thought to have low relevance in their countries" (this particularly applied to Japan) and that "schizophrenia and other nonaffective psychoses, although important mental disorders, were not included in the core WMH assessment."

These admissions provide some explanation for why the WMH found prevalence to be unusually low in several European countries. Note that only Europe was affected—the ICPE and WMH gave similar estimates for the USA and Mexico.

This is highly significant because Wilkinson and Pickett rely entirely on the WMH study for their European figures. All the figures for the less equal English-speaking nations are drawn from elsewhere. At the very least, this is comparing apples with oranges. Although there are simply not enough studies for us to compare rates of mental illness with any confidence, a reasonable approach would be to exclude the WMH figures and look at the rest. If we do this, a very different picture emerges to the one shown in *The Spirit Level* (see figure 2.4).[16]

The figures for Finland and Norway were available when Wilkinson and Pickett wrote *The Spirit Level*. Perhaps they were unaware of them, but they were certainly aware of the Singapore study, since it was included in the graph they created for *Affluenza*.[17]

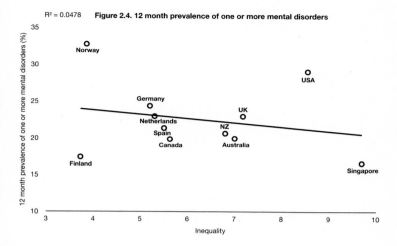

$R^2 = 0.0478$ **Figure 2.4. 12 month prevalence of one or more mental disorders**

The scarcity of data means that this graph makes no claim to be definitive, but studies of specific mental disorders suggest that it provides a more accurate picture than that shown in *The Spirit Level*. The most striking feature of the literature on psychiatric epidemiology is how little variation exists from country to country. The percentage of people suffering from major depression in any 12 month period is consistently found to be 5-10%[18] throughout Europe, Australia and North America. Rates of generalised anxiety disorder are consistently reported within the narrow range of 1-3%[19] and bipolar disorder typically affects 0.5-1.5% of the population.

If the inequality hypothesis is correct, the egalitarian Nordic states should have very low rates of mental disorder. This, however, is not the case. Far from having better mental health, the Nordic states find themselves at the upper end of these ranges. A 2000 study reported a rate of 9.3% for major depression in Finland,[20] putting it above the USA[21] (8.7%) and Canada[22] (8.2%) as well as being above the European Union average (8.3%).[23] With over 6% of their citizens clinically dependent on alcohol—double the EU average—Sweden and

41

Norway hold the dubious honour of having the highest rates of alcoholism in Europe.[24]

A 2001 study of mental illness in the Norwegian capital Oslo found that more than half of its residents had a history of mental illness and that 32.8% had suffered a mental disorder in the past year. If this finding was reflected in the rest of Norway*, it would put the country above even the USA in the graph printed in *The Spirit Level*. Comparing their detailed findings with those of a similar American study, the Norwegian researchers reported "almost identical rates for alcohol abuse, major depression, and social phobia in the two countries."[25]

Those sentiments were echoed in 2006 by the authors of an extensive Scandinavian study of patients with generalised anxiety disorder and major depression, who wrote:

Overall, it can be concluded that the prevalence rate of generalized anxiety disorder and major depression in different European countries, including Denmark, Finland, Norway, and Sweden, are as high as those found in the United States.[26]

With the weight of evidence indicating that rates of mental disorder do not vary significantly throughout North America and Europe, Japan is left to shoulder the responsibility of propping up the inequality theory. Its low figure of 8.8% also comes from the WMH study which, as we have seen, has a tendency to understate rates of mental disorder. But even if it is accurate, there is no suggestion that Japan's narrower gap between rich and poor is responsible. The same study finds a similar rate in China (9.1%) and notes that "consistent with previous research... prevalence is low in Asian countries."[30]

---

* Although it seems likely that the capital city would have higher rates of mental disorder than the rest of the country, this is not necessarily so. Norway has been found to have even higher rates of depression in rural areas than in urban areas.[27] The rates found in Oslo are very similar to those found in New York City.[28] A 1984 study found mental disorder prevalence in urban Sweden to be an incredible 47%.[29]

The psychiatric revolution

Some readers will not feel comforted by the news that around a quarter of the population has suffered from mental illness in the last year. It should be said, however, that at least half of these cases are mild. In Britain, for example, by far the most common 'mental disorders' are fatigue, sleeplessness and irritability. Many others may simply not exist.

The expansion of the psychiatric industry and the widening of the definition of emotional distress provide much of the explanation for why so many people are now diagnosed with mental problems. At the end of the 1970s, two developments in the way mental disorders were measured made an epidemic in the next decade virtually inevitable.

Firstly, the psychiatric establishment began to greatly expand the definition of mental illness. In 1974, the American Psychiatric Association began revising its *Diagnostic and Statistical Manual of Mental Disorders* (DSM). Dr Robert Spitzer, an influential psychiatrist from Columbia University, was put in charge of a task force to create a new edition of this psychiatric text-book. The DSM had first been published in 1952. At that time it ran to 130 pages and included 106 mental disorders. The second edition (DSM-II) appeared in 1968 and added a further 82 disorders.

With Spitzer at the helm, the number of disorders expanded further still. When DSM-III was finally published in 1980, it ran to 494 pages and contained no fewer than 265 separate mental disorders, but its size only hinted at the seismic shift the DSM-III represented.

Previous editions had described disorders but left psychiatrists to diagnose patients in their own way. It was a subjective system in an age that demanded objectivity and huge inconsistencies in diagnosis followed as a result. There was no uniformity from one practitioner to another, let alone from one country to another. British psychiatrists, for example, were diagnosing depression five times more often than their American counterparts.

This came at a time when psychiatry was having to defend itself from critics who questioned its legitimacy and accused it of being a tool of social control. In a famous experiment, David Rosenhan sent eight sane volunteers to five psychiatric hospitals, instructing them to say that they heard a word in their head but to otherwise act normally. The hospitals diagnosed all of them with mental illness and locked them up, some for several months. After Rosenhan made the experiment public, another hospital boasted that it would have spotted the frauds. Rosenhan responded by promising to send more volunteers to test them. Three months later, the hospital declared 41 of its 193 patients to be impostors, with a further 42 deemed 'suspect'. Rosenhan triumphantly announced that he had sent no one.[31]

In the wake of embarrassments such as this, Spitzer resolved to write a reliable manual which would help psychiatrists make consistent diagnoses. To this end, DSM-III provided lists of symptoms for each disorder. If a patient exhibited a number of these symptoms, he could be diagnosed as mentally unwell. This development was warmly welcomed by lawyers and insurance companies who now had a means of testing whether claimants were genuinely sick or not. More ominously, it was welcomed by those in the pharmaceutical industry who needed a list of *bona fide* medical symptoms for their drugs to treat.

There is no suggestion that any of these industries put pressure on Spitzer to introduce a symptom-based system, rather it was a pragmatic response to a genuine problem. But, as has been said of DSM-III, "even a justified revolution has some unwarranted casualties."[32] The problem was that many of the symptoms were commonplace emotions that were experienced universally as a response to normal stress, heartache and misfortune. So long as a psychiatrist was present to ask the questions, these emotions could be understood in the context of the patient's life. But DSM-III soon fell into the hands of advertisers, drug companies and epidemiologists who asked the questions without looking for the context. DSM-III made it possible for anyone to diagnose a disorder by asking straight-forward questions such as:

Has there ever been two weeks or more when you lost interest in most things like work, hobbies, or things you usually liked to do?

Since many symptoms listed in DSM-III were neither severe nor rare, the number of people who could be termed mentally ill spiralled upwards. The check-list of symptoms made it possible to diagnose mental illness by questionnaire or over the telephone.

Encouraged by pharmaceutical and psychiatric advertising, particularly in the USA, people began to diagnose themselves. Individuals who would never have previously been classified as mentally ill began diagnosing their shyness as social phobia and their sleeplessness as generalised anxiety disorder. This wave of induced panic drove hoards of self-diagnosed patients into the arms of psychiatrists and onto mind-altering drugs such as Fluoexetine. Better known as *Prozac*, this antidepressant was selling to the tune of $3 billion a year by the mid-1990s and was being prescribed not just for depression but for panic disorder, obsessive-compulsive disorder and social anxiety disorder.

Most significantly, from our point of view, the check-lists made it possible to diagnose mental disorders using epidemiological surveys. This was the second major development of the psychiatric revolution.

In the early 1980s, rather than waiting for people to visit the psychiatrist, the US National Institute of Mental Health began surveying the population at random, with simple yes/no questions based on the new criteria for emotional distress. Unsurprisingly, the number of people suffering from the broad range of mental disorders was much greater than anyone had previously suspected. Further studies in the USA and elsewhere used similar methodology and came to the same conclusion: there was an epidemic of mental illness.

The surveys seemed to show that millions of people were mentally ill without knowing it. Rather than taking this as a sign that DSM-III was encouraging an excessively liberal definition of mental illness, it was seen as proof that there was a huge unmet need for psychiatric care in the population. Since these untreated cases had failed to seek help, they must not have realised that they had a problem. Consequently, a vast advertising and screening effort was launched in order to get the public to own up to having mental disorders they weren't aware of. Such was the logic of the psychiatric establishment.

When, in *Affluenza*, Oliver James writes "say what you like about psychiatrists, but they are good at measuring depression," he ignores the fact that psychiatrists are not measuring depression, or anything else, in the surveys upon which he relies. For the most part, psychiatrists have never even met these people. Instead, the surveys are conducted by lay interviewers who ask people questions such as whether they are "much more talkative," "more interested in sex" or "much more active" than usual.

The interviewee's yes/no responses are then fed into a computer which tallies them against the ever-expanding list of traumas, syndromes and addictions listed in DSM-III or, since 1994, the doorstep-like DSM-IV. This list includes such disorders as borderline personality disorder, post-traumatic stress disorder, attention deficit hyperactivity disorder, manic-depression, chronic fatigue syndrome, generalised anxiety disorder, social phobia, codependency, multiple personality disorder, childhood stress, adult ADHD, recovering alcoholism, obsessive compulsive disorder, sex addiction and fibromyalgia.

These surveys did not so much monitor the epidemic of mental illness as create it. As Dr Jerome Wakefield says:

"By using checklists of symptoms you have gone out and confused normal human responses to life with mental disorder and therefore created an illusion of a vast epidemic; a medicalised illusion."[33]

It is now widely accepted, even by those who were most closely involved with the psychiatric revolution, that the 'epidemic' of mental illness which began around 1980 was largely a statistical phenomenon created by the radical change in psychiatry represented by DSM-III and the simplistic, symptom-based surveys that accompanied it.

In 2007, Dr Wakefield, along with Dr Allan Horwitz, published *The Loss of Sadness: How Psychiatry Transformed Normal Sorrow Into Depressive Disorder*. As its title suggests, the book argues that the psychiatric establishment has for years been wrongly classifying those with legitimate reasons for sorrow as suffering from major depressive disorder. It is, they say, this tendency to diagnose those who have been passed over for promotion or lost a pet as clinically depressed that explains the supposed rise of depression in the West, and in the USA in particular.

This critique—one of many—was given greater weight by the support of Dr Robert Spitzer, the architect of DSM-III, who wrote the foreword to the book, saying:

Dr Wakefield has critiqued my efforts in ways that I have largely become convinced are valid... [DSM-III's] diagnostic criteria specified the symptoms that must be present to justify a given diagnosis, but ignored any reference to the context in which they developed. In so doing, they allowed normal responses to stressors to be characterised as symptoms of disorder.

Spitzer was at pains to point out that DSM-III was designed to be used by psychiatrists to diagnose patients who came to see them, not to screen the general population at random:

The researchers who have conducted the epidemiological studies over the past two decades have totally ignored this problem. The result has been semiofficial prevalence rates that many find unbelievable.[34]

All of this—the contradictory studies, the redefinition of mental illness, Spitzer's *mea culpa,* and the vested financial interests of the pharmaceutical and psychiatric industries who benefited from medicalising human emotions—place a huge question mark over the surveys upon which Oliver James' hypothesis depends, and yet there is no mention of it in *Affluenza* or *The Selfish Capitalist.* Nor is there any mention of the crucial point that, while the new methods of the late 1970s created implausibly high estimates of mental illness, these estimates have not risen significantly since, despite growing inequality.[35]

For James, the only point of interest is that the psychiatric revolution happened to coincide with the election of Thatcher and Reagan. The resulting mental health prevalence figures can therefore be attributed to their economic policies. This would be a remarkably flimsy basis on which to base a solitary article in an obscure journal, let alone two best-selling books.[36]

As for the inequality hypothesis put forward in *The Spirit Level,* it is clear that virtually all the international literature on psychiatric epidemiology (patchy though it is) indicates that rates of emotional distress do not vary significantly from one wealthy country to another. Only by making selective use of the data is it possible to argue otherwise.

There is no credible evidence that people in more egalitarian countries have better mental health.

3

The pursuit of happiness

"We find ourselves anxiety-ridden, prone to depression, worried about
how others see us, unsure of our friendships, driven to consume
and with little or no community life."
— *The Spirit Level* (p. 3)

But what's it all worth, if we are not happy? The ultimate
measure of whether a society is 'doing better' lies in the
happiness of its people. Despite Oliver James' rejection of the
very concept, *The Spirit Level* argues that happiness does exist, is
important and is in short supply in unequal countries.

For their analysis, Wilkinson and Pickett were influenced
by the ideas of the economist Richard Layard (now Baron
Layard of Highgate) and his book *Happiness: Lessons from a New
Science*. Layard called for a happiness index to replace gross
national product as the barometer of a country's progress.
Economic growth, he said, was no longer making us happier and
the excessive wealth of a minority was inflicting misery upon the
less fortunate. Like Wilkinson and Pickett, Layard fully believes
that inequality has damaging 'psychosocial' effects for which the
wealthy must be held accountable.

If a person works harder and earns more, he may himself gain by increasing his
income compared with other people. But the other people lose because their

income now falls relative to his. He does not care that he is polluting other people this way."[1]

The answer to this 'pollution', says Layard, is to tax the rich. By paying higher taxes, the rich can compensate for the damage they are doing to the psyches of the less well-off; psyches that are no less damaged by the fact that they, too, are becoming wealthier. The rich would themselves benefit from this approach, says Layard, since higher taxes will deter them from working too hard, thereby encouraging them to spend more time with their family.

Since they also favour greater redistribution, Wilkinson and Pickett are favourably disposed to Layard's view of inequality as a negative externality and they, too, begin their book by comparing levels of happiness from country to country. For this, they turned to the World Values Survey.

Measuring happiness

The simplest way of finding out if someone is happy is to ask them. The World Values Survey has been asking people this question for decades, giving them four options: 'very happy', 'quite happy', 'not very happy' and 'not at all happy'. By this measure, as Layard shows in his book, levels of happiness in developed countries have barely changed since 1960.

Layard, James and Wilkinson & Pickett all refer to the World Values Survey data on happiness. Considering the subject matter of these books it would be odd if they did not. But while they are central to Layard's thesis, James describes them as "worthless". His objection is that happiness means different things in different countries, and that some cultures encourage people to say they're happy when they're not (and vice versa).

He might have a point. The people of China and Hong Kong, for example, seem less willing to declare themselves happy than citizens of other countries. It is certainly plausible that the

Japanese would make less of a show of their inner joy than Americans. On the other hand, these surveys also find that immigrants declare themselves as happy as the host population, indicating that the culture they come from has less bearing than their current environment.

On balance, sociologists have concluded that whilst some cultures do not distinguish between depression and sadness, 'happiness' means much the same thing everywhere. Certainly all cultures can distinguish it from unhappiness. And even if cultural differences skew results between continents, there is less reason to think that they would do so between European countries. James' distrust of the happiness surveys more likely stems from the fact that they stubbornly fail to support either of his two pet theories: that people are less happy now than in the past, and that unequal countries are less happy than equal ones.

Layard's core ideas are more restrained than those put forward in *Affluenza* and *The Spirit Level*. While those books argue that life is getting worse in unequal countries, Layard merely believes that things are not getting much better. Happiness, he says, has remained constant *despite* economic growth. This is not a new theory. In economics, it is known as the Easterlin Paradox, after Richard Easterlin who, in 1974, argued that once countries reached a high level of development, further growth did not make them significantly happier.[2]

In recent years, the Easterlin Paradox has been challenged by economists who say that there is evidence that economic growth does indeed continue to increase happiness.[3] The rights and wrongs of that debate need not concern us here. It is sufficient to know that while Layard accepts the orthodox view of flat-lining happiness in rich countries, at no point does he claim that rich countries have become *less* happy. Quite the reverse:

In the West we have a society that is probably as happy as any there has ever been.[4]

And he explicitly rules out economic growth as a cause of society's malaise:

> Economic growth as such provides no explanation, because economic growth has occurred for the last 150 years, but family break-up, higher crime and weaker moral values are a feature of only the last fifty.[5]

Having accepted that happiness has remained constant for decades, Layard's objective is to not allow it to fall and, if possible, to make people even happier.

Wilkinson and Pickett's inequality hypothesis is profoundly different. By their reckoning, people are happier in more equal countries while those in the supposedly anxious, lonely and atomised unequal countries are getting more miserable. The World Values Survey happiness figures do not support this theory. If inequality caused unhappiness, this should be reflected in countries like Britain and the USA which have become less equal over time. There is little evidence for this, but the two epidemiologists do not discard the happiness surveys altogether. Instead, they put them to brief use in a way that superficially supports their argument.

Figure 3.1 shows gross national income (GNI) per capita against the percentage of people saying they are 'very happy' or 'quite happy'. A very similar graph appears in both *Happiness* and *The Spirit Level*, although figure 3.1 uses slightly more recent data.[6]

This graph tells us two things. Firstly, it is quite possible to be poor but happy; countries like Indonesia, Malaysia and Brazil show us that. Secondly, you are much more likely to be happy if you live in a wealthy country; none of the countries with a national income above $35,000 have fewer than 82% of their population reporting happiness. Money doesn't buy you happiness, but it seems to help.

Wilkinson and Pickett put a different spin on this graph. They claim that it "shows the 'happiness curve' levelling off in the richest countries in much the same way as life expectancy."[7]

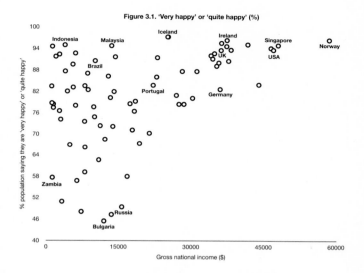

Figure 3.1. 'Very happy' or 'quite happy' (%)

This is true, but the reason is not hard to fathom. Look at the top of the graph. All the richest countries are very nearly at 100% happiness. What socialist miracle do Wilkinson and Pickett have in mind that would propel happiness beyond the 100% that would be required for the curve to keep rising?

The happiness graph and the life expectancy graph do indeed have much in common. Just as there is a biological limit to how far we can expect life expectancy to rise, so there is a mathematical limit on how far happiness can rise. There might be some debate about the realistic limit of human longevity, but happiness cannot rise above 100% and no one argues that money can guarantee happiness for everyone.

Having dug out the World Values Survey to show the levels of happiness for dozens of countries against income, you might expect Wilkinson and Pickett to draw up another graph showing happiness against inequality. Considering the overall 'equal societies are happier' hypothesis, it's hard to believe such a graph does not appear. It should show a downward trend, with the most equal countries having the highest scores and the least equal countries having the lowest. As you can see from figure 3.2 this is not what happens at all. Some of the Southern European countries have somewhat lower scores, as do Hungary and Slovenia, but there is no correlation with inequality.[8]

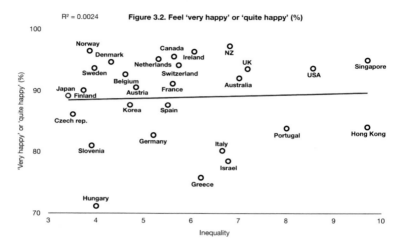

Figure 3.2. Feel 'very happy' or 'quite happy' (%)

There is, however, a clear correlation with income. Figure 3.3 uses the same data as figure 3.1 but focuses on the richest countries and their gross national incomes.[9] It shows that, even for the wealthiest nations, happiness grows in line with income. It suggests that although countries such as Italy, Greece, Israel and Slovenia are rich by international standards, further economic growth could make them as happy as the Ireland, Norway or Canada.

These graphs undermine the central premise of *The Spirit Level*. Even at a very high level of development, countries *can* still benefit from economic growth. Eventually, of course, there is a limit, but that limit seems only to be reached when 95% of the population declare themselves 'quite happy' or 'very happy'.

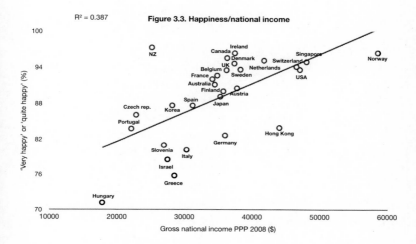

Figure 3.3. Happiness/national income

But what if Oliver James is correct and the happiness index is unreliable? Can we measure happiness in other ways? Richard Layard believes so. In *Happiness*, Layard set out seven criteria ('the Big Seven') which are most important in creating happiness.

Two of these—financial situation and health—have already been discussed, insofar as they can be measured by income and life expectancy. Two others—personal freedom and personal values—are almost impossible to quantify, although there is no doubt that having goals and having the freedom to work towards them make us happier.

Layard's other criteria are community life, family relationships and work. International comparisons for these aspects of happiness can be measured by the World Values Survey.

Community life

Amongst the World Values Survey findings are data showing how many people are involved in local sports, religious, charity and arts groups. This should give us an idea of how involved people are in their community. Figure 3.4 shows this data.[10] (This is an average—the total number of people participating will be much higher, but since some people are involved in two or more groups we cannot simply add them together.)

The graph shows that, on the whole, those in more equal societies are less inclined to be involved in community groups than those in less equal countries.

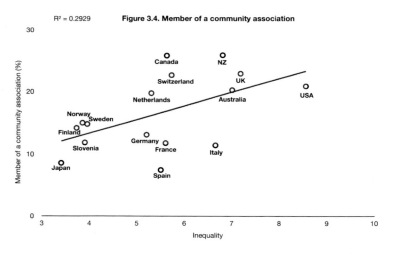

$R^2 = 0.2929$ Figure 3.4. Member of a community association

Because the index includes religious organisations, you might think this discriminates in favour of the USA, where church attendance is unusually high. To see if this is the case, figure 3.5 shows the same data but excludes religion.[11] Sure enough, the USA drops down but the general trend remains (by excluding religion, it could be argued that we are discriminating against the USA, since if these believers were not involved in the church

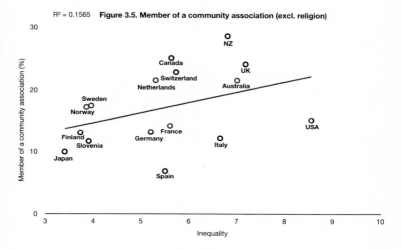

$R^2 = 0.1565$ **Figure 3.5. Member of a community association (excl. religion)**

some of them would surely be involved in other community activities).

There is no evidence that people in egalitarian countries are more likely to join other types of clubs or associations. Americans, for example, are far more likely to be actively involved in politics (16.3%) than in Sweden (2.8%) or Japan (2.1%). People in less equal countries are also more likely to join environmental organisations. More than 6% of the population of the USA, UK and Canada are actively involved in environmental groups, compared with less than 2% in Scandinavian countries.

The only area in which more equal countries tend to score higher is in trade union membership, but even here the proportion of people who are *actively* involved is higher in the USA than in many European countries. Trade union membership is, in any case, a poor indicator of social capital since it is often strongly encouraged, if not compulsory, in certain industries.

Trust

Another measure of 'community spirit' is how trusting people are of each other. This is the aspect Wilkinson and Pickett focus on in their chapter on 'community life and social relations' and it is crucial to their overall hypothesis. The World Values Survey holds information on how many people agree with the statement 'can most people be trusted?' Wilkinson and Pickett argue that this data show that people are more trusting in more equal countries. Unfortunately, some of the data they use are fifteen years old and do not give a reliable picture of current trends. Figure 3.6 shows the latest available data, although this does not greatly alter the overall picture.[12]

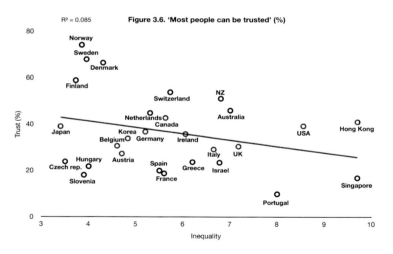

Figure 3.6. 'Most people can be trusted' (%)

There appears to be a correlation between trust and income equality here, but it is solely due by the four Nordic countries being significantly more trusting. Exclude them and the correlation disappears. The other 24 countries do not follow the gradient at all and a number of very unequal countries—New Zealand, Australia, Hong Kong and the USA—score well above average. When only 4 out of 28 countries follow the 'trend', there is no trend. There may be a good reason why self-reported levels of trust are higher in Scandinavia (possibly related to its ethnic homogeneity[13]), but the evidence from the other countries suggests that it has nothing to do with income equality. To say, as Wilkinson and Pickett do, that this data prove that more equal countries are six times more trusting than unequal countries is a gross distortion.

It should be mentioned—since Wilkinson and Pickett do not—that the World Values Survey gives only two options in its question about trust. The first is 'most people can be trusted'. The second option is not 'no one can be trusted' or even 'most people cannot be trusted', but merely 'you can't be too careful'. This is a rather equivocal answer and it is quite possible to agree with both statements at the same time. At the very least, it should be recognised that being cautious when dealing with strangers is not the same thing as being deeply mistrustful of society as a whole or being withdrawn from community life.

Nevertheless, the importance of this graph to Wilkinson and Pickett's hypothesis cannot be overstated. For them, it is the killer proof that people in less equal societies are suspicious, insecure and lack a sense of community. These are the 'psychosocial pathways' which cause virtually every health and social problem and Wilkinson and Pickett refer to them throughout *The Spirit Level*. Focusing on the Portuguese figure, they write: "Imagine living somewhere where 90 per cent of the population mistrusts one another and what that must mean for the quality of everyday life."[14] By their closing chapters, they are talking about "a society where you must be prepared to treat others with suspicion, watch your back and fight for what you can get."[15] Although this message is repeated *ad nauseum* throughout *The Spirit Level*, it is important to remember that the main evidence for it comes from the ambiguous data shown in figure 3.6.

Family relationships

Layard emphasises the importance of family life in generating happiness. By his reckoning, being divorced makes people twice as unhappy as they would be from losing a third of their income. Fellow economists Blanchflower and Oswald estimated that a lasting marriage is worth $100,000 a year in well-being.[16] Being raised by two parents is also beneficial. Layard provides figures showing that those who are raised by a single parent are far more likely to have a criminal record by the time they leave home and are less likely to have a college degree or find employment.

Wilkinson and Pickett do not mention this aspect of happiness but it is clear from figure 3.7 that divorce is no more common in unequal countries than elsewhere.[17] There is even some suggestion of an inverse correlation, although this is largely due to lower divorce rates in Southern Europe.

The story is somewhat different when it comes to the number of teenagers having babies. Here, there does seem to be a correlation with inequality. Wilkinson and Pickett use data

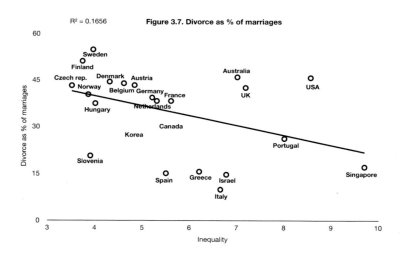

$R^2 = 0.1656$

Figure 3.7. Divorce as % of marriages

from UNICEF's *League Table of Teenage Births in Rich Countries* to create this graph. Figure 3.8 recreates it using the same data. Figures for Singapore, Hong Kong, Slovenia and Israel are not available from the UNICEF report and come from the United Nations Population Fund report.[18]

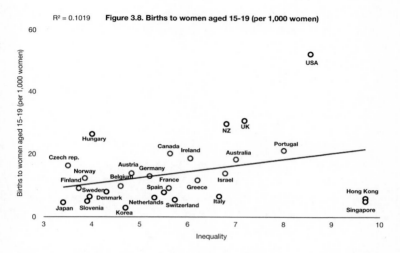

$R^2 = 0.1019$ **Figure 3.8. Births to women aged 15-19 (per 1,000 women)**

Wilkinson and Pickett claim that "there is a strong tendency for more unequal countries and more unequal states to have higher teenage birth rates—much too strong to be attributable to chance."[19] The authors of the UNICEF report make no such assertion. They explicitly reject the possibility of a single unifying explanation for why teen birth rates vary, saying "teenage birth rates are the result of a complex interplay of forces, and there is no one equation that can adequately explain or predict their outcome."[20]

Wilkinson and Pickett seem unable to look beyond inequality for an explanation, and so, for example, when they say that teen births are twice as high in Mississippi than Utah, they put it down to inequality. A far more likely explanation is that 60% of Utah's population belong to the strict Mormon religion.

There are many cultural, historical and religious reasons why teen birth rates vary between countries. Teen births have declined sharply in every rich nation (bar Ireland and Japan) in the last 40 years, and some have seen bigger drops than others. Most countries have seen rates fall by half and some by three-quarters as a result of greater access to contraception and people marrying later in life.

Australia, New Zealand and Canada have more than halved their teen birth rate since 1970, so it is hard to argue that inequality is the main cause of teen pregnancy. To put it another way, these countries had *very* high rates of teen pregnancy 40 years ago when the gap between rich and poor was narrower. If New Zealand's rate of 29.8 births per 1,000 looks high now, bear in mind that it was once 64.3 per 1,000.[21]

In 1970, however, many more teen births took place within wedlock and having children at a young age was not perceived to be a problem so long as the woman was married. The general trend towards marrying later has reduced the teen birth rate in nearly all developed countries but teen marriages remain common in some places. Portugal's teen birth rate is relatively high, but these teenagers are four times more likely to be married than Norwegians or Britons. Abortion was also illegal in Portugal until 2007; a significant fact which does not warrant a mention in *The Spirit Level*.[22]

Nonetheless, it is true that Britain, New Zealand and the USA have not seen their teen birth rates fall as sharply as most other countries, and, since they are both 'unequal', this fact would seem to support Wilkinson and Pickett's hypothesis.

There is no question that relative poverty is associated with teenage pregnancies. Young women with few qualifications and a poor education are more likely to both get pregnant and to have the baby, particularly when they know they will receive financial support from the state.

But it is also true that teenage pregnancies *create* relative poverty. Studies have shown that even when social class and education are taken into account, women who have babies in their teenage years are less likely to own their own home, to be in employment or to live in an affluent area.[23] The relationship between poverty and teen pregnancies is self-perpetuating and Wilkinson and Pickett's term 'recycling deprivation' is apt, all the more so since women who have children early in life tend to have more children overall.

The authors of the UNICEF document recognise the association between relative poverty and teen births, and they also recognise that the cause-and-effect cuts both ways. Unlike Wilkinson and Pickett, they do not claim that inequality is the main driver of high teen births; if it was, Switzerland, Singapore and Italy would have much higher rates. Instead, the authors emphasise the importance of traditional values and sex education.

One of the keys to interpreting the league table of teenage birth rates therefore seems to be that countries with low teenage birth rates tend to be *either* countries that have travelled less far from traditional values *or* countries which have embraced the socio-sexual transformation *but have also taken steps to equip their young people to cope with it.* (Italics in the original)[24]

Japan and Korea fall into the first category. In these countries, traditional values remain strong and society tends to frown on unmarried teenagers getting pregnant. Such sentiments may have waned in Britain and the USA but, since they remain strong in countries such as Italy and Singapore, it is tenuous to argue that inequality is responsible for bringing about this cultural change.

Sweden and the Netherlands fall into the second category. They have both made concerted efforts to adapt to changes in sexual behavior (ie. more teenagers having sex more often). By talking openly about sex and contraception from an early age— both at home and in school—they have removed much of the stigma and embarrassment from the subject. Attempts to do likewise in the Anglo-Saxon nations have met with resistance, particularly from the religious right.

Attitudes towards abortion also vary from country to country. In the Nordic states, abortion is effectively used as a form of birth control. 70% of all teen pregnancies in Denmark and Sweden end in termination, compared to less than half in the UK, New Zealand and the USA. Abortion remains one of the most divisive issues in American politics and moral objections to abortion inevitably have an effect on the number of teen births.[25] Again, these primarily religious objections cannot be linked to inequality.

Having a baby at a young age by no means condemns the child to a life of unemployment and crime. From a biological perspective, having children early in life is natural and healthy. The problems associated with teen births today are not medical but socio-economic; how the child is brought up is more important than the age of the mother.

Figure 3.9 shows the percentage of children who live in single parent households.[26] Again, there is no correlation with inequality. Sweden, the UK and the USA have the largest

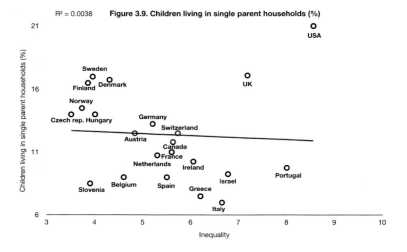

$R^2 = 0.0038$ **Figure 3.9. Children living in single parent households (%)**

number of single-parent households, closely followed by the rest of Scandinavia. Data are not available for New Zealand and Australia, but considering their high divorce and teen birth rates, it is fair to guess that they will be around the same mark as the UK.

Taking rates of divorce, teen births and single parents together, there is no consistent link with inequality. More equal countries tend to have fewer teen births (which is what Wilkinson and Pickett focus on), but do rather worse in terms of the number of broken homes and lone parents. If, as Layard contends, these factors are important for generating happiness, more equal countries are no happier than others.

Work

Layard's third criterion for happiness is gainful employment. Work gives the individual money and a sense of purpose. It is, therefore, doubly important in creating well-being. Conversely, unemployment is a great source of unhappiness. As Layard says, unemployment "reduces income but it also reduces happiness directly by destroying the self-respect and social relationships created by work."[27]

The success of an economy can justifiably be measured by its unemployment rate, since no other measure has so devastating an effect on the individual. This was one of J.K. Galbraith's key arguments in *The Affluent Society* (1958). Galbraith's critique of consumerism is often cited by the left, but they rarely quote the following passage from his revised introduction (written in 1984), in which he explains that inequality is of little concern to people unless they find themselves without a job:

When, as suggested in this book, men and women are employed and at continuously improving wages or salaries, they are not greatly concerned that others, with whatever justification or absence of justification, have more, even greatly more.

The relevant comparison is not with what others have but with one's own previous economic position—it is the improvement over the previous year that is noticed. When unemployment, wage reductions and wage give-backs are endemic, the comparison with previous years is unfavourable. Then the mind turns to the better fortune of the fortunate. Inequality regains its standing as an issue.[28]

Unemployment is, therefore, a useful measure of an economy's effectiveness and of society's happiness. Figure 3.10 shows the average rate of unemployment between 1995 and 2005. This graph uses the long-term average from the UN's Human Development Report to avoid temporary blips and anomalies.[29] The most striking aspect is the high rate of unemployment in Southern Europe and the low rate in the USA. Plainly, there is no association with inequality.

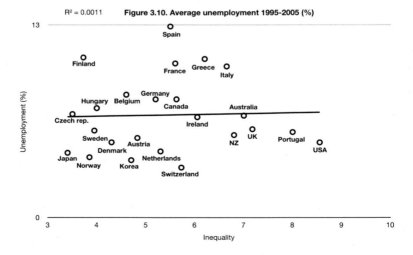

Figure 3.10. Average unemployment 1995-2005 (%)

A better explanation for the variation between countries lies in their respective welfare systems, as Layard explained in a 2001 paper:

Europe has a notorious unemployment problem. But if you break down unemployment into short-term (under a year) and long-term, you find that short-term unemployment is almost the same in Europe as in the U.S. – around 4% of the workforce. But in Europe there are another 4% who have been out of work for over a year, compared with almost none in the United States. The most obvious explanation for this is that in the U.S. unemployment benefits run out after 6 months, while in most of Europe they continue for many years or indefinitely.[30]

Since long-term unemployment is far more damaging to self-esteem than short-term unemployment, countries with a less generous welfare system can be seen to benefit by disincentivising worklessness. Certainly, as the graph shows, social democratic countries are no more capable of reducing unemployment than less equal nations. If low unemployment is a measure of happiness, they are no happier.

Quality of life

Tying together all the strands of what makes us happy is no easy task. Although Layard calls happiness studies a 'new science', it remains largely subjective. Nonetheless, Layard's criteria for happiness possess a certain logic and have much to commend them.

The best attempt to create an objective happiness index is the Economist Intelligence Unit's quality-of-life index. This is made up of seven criteria which are similar to Layard's Big Seven. The only major difference is the replacement of the rather vague 'personal values' with gender equality (measured by the pay gap between the sexes). The criteria are material well-being, health, family relations, job security, social and community activities, political freedom and gender equality.

Figure 3.11 shows the quality-of-life index plotted against rates of inequality.

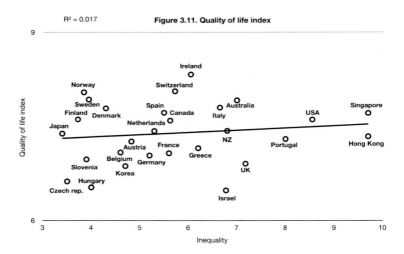

$R^2 = 0.017$ **Figure 3.11. Quality of life index**

As with the World Values Survey happiness index, there is no association. The index's compilers even went to the trouble of addressing the inequality hypothesis head on:

There is no evidence for an explanation sometimes proffered for the apparent paradox of increasing incomes and stagnant life-satisfaction scores: the idea that an increase in someone's income causes envy and reduces the welfare and satisfaction of others. In our estimates, the level of income inequality had no impact on levels of life satisfaction.[31]

In summary, more equal societies are not happier than less equal societies. This is evident from subjective tests (asking people how happy they are) and in objective tests (the quality-of-life index).

The criteria examined in this chapter do much more than merely tell us whether people are feeling upbeat or not.

Employment, income, family, health and community life are at the very heart of how we judge the social and economic success of a nation. If more equal countries 'almost always do better' we would expect to see evidence of it here. That we do not is a serious blow to the inequality hypothesis.

Before leaving the subject of happiness, there is one last way of comparing levels of happiness between countries. Figure 3.12 shows the suicide rate per 100,000 matched, as usual, against inequality. Here, we see a clear inverse correlation which, as Wilkinson and Pickett might say, cannot be attributed to chance. Eleven of the twelve countries with the highest suicide rates are 'more equal' (Hong Kong is the exception). Although Sweden's reputation for having an exceptionally high rate of suicide is not particularly well deserved, Swedes are still twice as likely to commit suicide than Britons. Finns are three times as likely to do so.

Although they do not show this graph in *The Spirit Level*, Wilkinson and Pickett mention the high rate of suicide in more

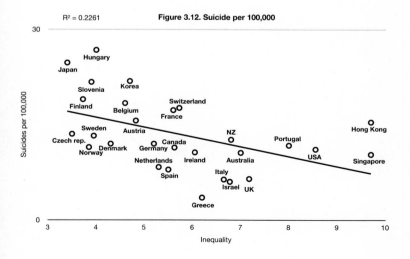

$R^2 = 0.2261$ **Figure 3.12. Suicide per 100,000**

equal societies, and come up with an extraordinary and novel explanation.

Some people, they say, take their anger out on others and some people direct their rage in on themselves. In more egalitarian societies people who feel frustration with life do the decent thing and kill themselves. In less equal countries, selfish capitalists express their anger by killing other people. This, they say, explains why the murder rate is so much higher in less equal societies.

It's a bizarre theory and would be a testament to the caring, sharing attitude that the redistribution of wealth engenders if it was true. But, as we shall see in the next chapter, it is not.

4

Crime and punishment

"The trend for more unequal countries to have
higher homicide rates is well established"
— claim made in *The Spirit Level* (p. 136)

The strongest graph in *The Spirit Level* shows rates of imprisonment against rates of inequality. Its strength lies in its consistency. Unlike most of the graphs in the book, the correlation is displayed by the full range of nations rather than a handful of special cases and outliers. It appears to show unequivocally that unequal countries send more people to prison. The rate in the USA is so high that they had to rescale to graph to fit it in.

Wilkinson and Pickett appear to have used data from 2000 to illustrate their point. Figure 4.1 shows prisoners per 100,000 in the most recent years for which UN data is available (2004 or earlier).[1] The trend remains much the same as in *The Spirit Level*. The USA is the obvious outlier and the Czech Republic and Hungary add a little balance at the other end, showing that low rates of imprisonment are by no means inevitable in more equal countries. However, even if these countries are excluded, the correlation between imprisonment and inequality remains.

71

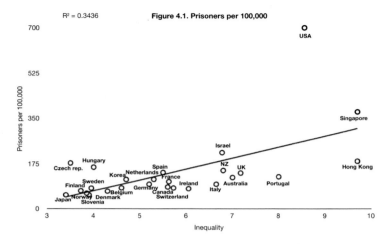

Figure 4.1. Prisoners per 100,000

But is it really a social problem? If a high imprisonment rate is indicative of a high crime rate, you may conclude that it is.[2] A high crime rate is surely indicative of a country not 'doing better'. If, on the other hand, a small prison population is the result of a lenient judicial system, rather than a dearth of crimes to prosecute, the desirability of half-empty prisons loses its allure.

In short, what is so wrong about sending criminals to prison? If your sympathy lies with the criminal, custodial sentences and longer prison terms are a bad thing. If you see the purpose of prison as being to punish and prevent crime, incarcerating criminals is desirable. In the final analysis, the measure of success lies in the crime rate, not the imprisonment rate.

Since the crime rate is such a key indicator of whether a country is 'doing better', it is odd that Wilkinson and Pickett pay so little attention to it. With the exception of homicide, crime is not included in their 'index of health and social problems'. That they title their chapter on the subject 'Imprisonment and Punishment' rather than the more usual

'Crime and Punishment' may indicate where their sympathies lie. Rather than looking at the crime rate, they focus on prison conditions and the supposed desirability of shorter sentences. They approvingly report that Japanese prisons have been described as "havens of tranquility" and say that prisons in the Netherlands are "characteristically humane and decent". Good news for criminals, but what about the law-abiding?

Figure 4.2 shows recorded crime per 100,000, according to the UN's Survey of Crime Trends.*[3] The results may surprise some readers. Egalitarian Sweden has the highest rate of recorded crime of any rich country. With 13,979 crimes per 100,000 people, its rate is more than three times higher than America's rate of 3,764 per 100,000. In fact, all the Scandinavian countries have a higher crime rate than the United States. Japan, on the other hand, has a very low crime rate, which suggests that it imprisons fewer people because there are fewer criminals to imprison. The Nordic states, on the other hand, *choose* to imprison fewer people. The result, it seems, is a higher crime rate.

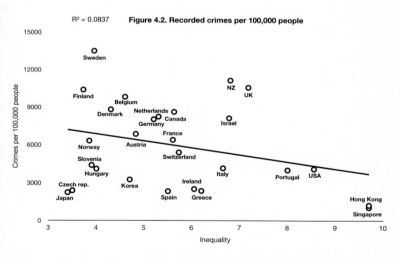

$R^2 = 0.0837$ **Figure 4.2. Recorded crimes per 100,000 people**

* Throughout this chapter, figures marked 'UK' are for England and Wales only.

It would be going too far to say that there is always an inverse correlation between imprisonment rates and crime rates, but there is a strong trend. The countries with the highest imprisonment rates—the Czech Republic, Portugal, the USA, Hong Kong and Singapore—have low crime rates. Israel is a slight exception as its crime rate is not particularly low, but it is still lower than that of liberal Finland and Sweden.

We are talking here about total recorded crime, but Sweden's position at the top of the pile is not due to speeding tickets and jay-walking. It has higher rates of theft (shown in figure 4.3), fraud, automobile theft and burglary than the USA, while the USA has higher rates of assault, robbery and drug offences.[4]

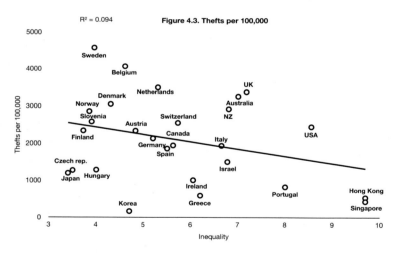

Figure 4.3. Thefts per 100,000

Because there are differences in the methods of recording crime from country to country, we should be wary of making direct comparisons. The graph above should be seen as suggestive rather than definitive, but the European Crime and Safety Survey provides corroborating evidence. Figure 4.4 shows the percentage of people who have been a victim of crime in the last

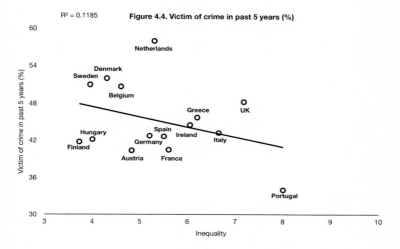

Figure 4.4. Victim of crime in past 5 years (%)

five years.[5] We can see that people's experience of crime largely reflects the recorded crime figures. While this survey only shows results for EU countries, it is sufficient for us to see that —at the very least—crime is not more common in less equal countries.

The overall crime rate hides a multitude of local differences. The Netherlands and Sweden both have high rates of bicycle theft, for example, while all the Nordic states have low levels of drug crime. Between those Nordic states, there is significant variation. The authors of the survey describe the crime rate in Finland as being "relatively low", Sweden's as being "medium to high" and Denmark's as being "high."[6]

Sweden and Denmark's victim-of-crime figures are above the EU average for robbery, theft from a car, motorcycle theft, sexual assault, hate crimes and fraud. Denmark has the second highest rate of burglary in the EU[7] but, interestingly, its population is the second least likely to expect a burglary.[8] Perceptions do not always match reality. It is a sad irony that the Swedes—who, of all EU citizens, are more likely to say that 'most people can be trusted'—are six times more likely to be sexually assaulted than the less trusting Portuguese.[9]

The high incidence of rape in Sweden is particularly surprising. The UN's figures for 2006 show the rate in Sweden to be 41 per 100,000 compared to 31 per 100,000 in the USA, a shocking statistic for a country which prides itself on its safety and gender equality.[10] And while incidence of rape is declining in America, it has doubled in the last decade in Sweden. According to the EU, it now stands at 46 per 100,000, the highest in Europe, as the Swedish press reported in 2009:

Sweden tops European rape league

In Sweden, 46 incidents of rape are reported per 100,000 residents. This figure is double as many as in the UK which reports 23 cases, and four times that of the other Nordic countries, Germany and France. The figure is up to 20 times the figure for certain countries in southern and eastern Europe.[11]

None of this should be taken as evidence that equality 'causes' crime. The wide variation between Scandinavian countries shows that many factors are at work. Assaults and drug offences remain more common in Anglo-Saxon nations and Britain continues to suffer very high rates of (drug related?) burglary.[12] What the crime surveys and the recorded crime figures *do* show is that inequality is totally unconnected with crime. The most crime-ridden countries in the European Crime and Safety Survey—the UK, Ireland, the Netherlands and Denmark—span the equality spectrum, as do the least affected: Hungary, Spain, France and Portugal. It is, however, worth noting that the supposedly less materialistic Scandinavian countries have high rates of property crime, theft and consumer fraud.

While there is no association between inequality and crime, there is substantial evidence that higher prison rates reduce criminality. There are, of course, downsides to having a large prison population. It is extremely costly and there is scant evidence that many offenders are ever successfully rehabilitated. Wilkinson and Pickett are almost certainly correct when they argue that too many Americans are sent to prison for minor offences. The absurd 'three strikes and you're out' law that exists in two dozen US states has filled prisons with minor offenders serving life sentences. Half of US prisoners are in jail for non-violent offences and America's obsessive war on drugs is arguably misguided. Many of its prisoners could be freed without a significant increase in crime ensuing.

Nevertheless, as long as drugs remain illegal, it is difficult to argue that the law should not be enforced. Harsh treatment of drug users is very much a feature of judicial policy in the USA and Singapore. But the war on drugs is not an inevitable consequence of inequality, just as high rates of imprisonment are not inevitable in unequal societies.

Nor is there anything inherently virtuous about *not* sending offenders to prison. Prison does seem to act as a deterrent in a way that the "programmes of education, training and recreation" favoured by Wilkinson and Pickett do not. It requires a perverse logic to argue that incarcerating criminals does not reduce the crime rate.

In the 1960s and 1970s, America had a far more liberal attitude to crime and punishment. The incarceration rate was lower in 1975 than it had been in 1960. This lenient approach coincided with a four-fold rise in crime, with the number of annual recorded offences rocketing from 3 million to 12 million.

Under the Reagan administration, things began to change. Conviction rates and custodial sentences increased sharply and longer prison terms were dished out. Much of this stemmed from the renewed war on drugs and although total recorded crime stabilised at around 13 million in the 1980s, the fifteen-fold increase in the number of drug offenders sent to prison did little to stem the rising tide of homicide, rape, robbery and assault.

In response to this epidemic of violent crime, the government took a still harder line. The prison population doubled between 1985 and 1994 and the crime wave finally came to an end. Incidence of rape, murder, robbery, burglary and assault all peaked between 1991 and 1993 and have been falling ever since. The overall crime rate declined from almost 10,000 crimes per 100,000 persons in 1995 to under 4,000 per 100,000 today.

Britain had a similar experience. Referring to the last fifteen years, Wilkinson and Pickett say: "Crime rates in the UK were falling as inexorably as imprisonment rates were rising" as if this highlighted the absurdity of Britain's judicial system, shutting the stable door after the horse had bolted. They never entertain the notion that falling rates of crime might have been the result of higher rates of imprisonment.[13]

Britain's experience closely echoed that of America's. Prison numbers barely changed between 1970 and the early 1990s.[14] In the same period, crime rose significantly.[15] Between 1981 and 1991, vehicle theft and burglary doubled. Robberies rose threefold. In 1993, following a huge rise in violent crime, the government launched a crack-down and prison numbers rose faster than at any time in the twentieth century. Almost immediately, the crime rate began to flatten out, peaking in 1995 before going into a nosedive.

Between 1995 and 2009, violent crime fell by half, vehicle-related thefts fell by 65%, domestic burglaries fell from 1,770,000 to 744,000, and vandalism fell by 18%. Overall, as prison numbers rose by 85%, crime fell by 45%, representing 9 million fewer crimes in 2009 than in 1995.[16]

It strains credibility to put all this down to serendipity. Of course, tougher sentencing was not the only reason for the drop in crime. A stronger economy, lower unemployment, improved security systems and better policing have all been put forward as contributing factors.

The economist Steven D. Levitt has controversially suggested that America's crime rate fell in the early 1990s as a result of abortion being legalised in 1973.[17] He argued that the crime-wave would have continued if the unwanted babies of the

1970s had been born and grown to adulthood. Instead, it ended at a time when the foetuses of 1973 would have been in their late teens and, therefore, at their criminal peak. By the same logic, Britain's crime-wave should have ended in the late 1980s (abortion was legalised in 1967). In fact the decline began at the same time as America's, in line with the flurry of jailings. Levitt himself concedes that increased imprisonment accounted for one third of the drop in crime.

Homicide

Wilkinson and Pickett say nothing about the contrast between the crime rate in countries which have a "characteristically humane" prison system and those which are "more punitive." The issue of crime is brushed over entirely, with the exception of homicide. Homicide rates in the USA remain higher than in other rich countries, largely as a result of widespread gun-ownership, drug wars, organised crime and gang violence.

For Wilkinson and Pickett, of course, the root cause of America's murder rate is inequality, but to demonstrate this they have to overcome an inconvenient fact. Like other crimes, America's homicide rate has been falling for nigh-on twenty years, with the decline being much steeper than in either Europe or neighbouring Canada. This is totally inconsistent with rising inequality.[18]

Faced with the awkward issue of a rapidly falling murder rate in a land of inequality, Wilkinson and Pickett admit that homicide rates in the US peaked in the early 1990s but claim that: "In 2005, they started to rise again."[19]

The first part is true enough. Homicide peaked in 1991 at 9.8 per 100,000. The second part is a hugely misleading. The "rise" they are referring to is a negligible blip from 5.5 to 5.6 per 100,000 recorded in 2005. Wilkinson and Pickett do not mention that this was a minor fluctuation in a downward trend, nor do they mention that by 2008 the homicide rate had fallen to 5.4 per 100,000, the lowest since 1965.[20]

Wilkinson and Pickett need the reader to buy into the idea that the murder rate is on the rise again because it fits their theory that American inequality peaked in the early 1990s, fell a little and then began rising again in 2000. This claim is mentioned nowhere else in *The Spirit Level* and is a rather surprising one since United Nations data show that inequality has steadily increased in America for many years. The source turns out to be a solitary discussion paper in an obscure journal which claims that, by one measure, inequality "increased steadily in the early 1990s, declined a little in the middle 1990s, and then rose sharply after 1996."[21] This idiosyncratic interpretation, even if true, is hardly sufficient to explain America's murder rate almost halving over two decades.

To demonstrate how inequality makes people murder one another, Wilkinson and Pickett show the average homicide rate from 1990 to 2000. The same United Nations data is shown in figure 4.4.[22]

According to Wilkinson and Pickett, "the trend for more unequal countries to have higher homicide rates is well

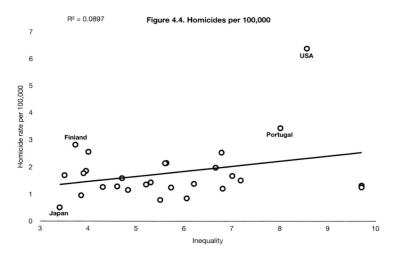

Figure 4.4. Homicides per 100,000

established." This is sheer fantasy. 26 of the 28 countries do not follow any pattern at all. Figure 4.4 highlights Portugal and the USA because it is their murder rate, and theirs alone, that props up the inequality hypothesis. Data from these two nations are not sufficient to justify the hyperbolic claim that the murder rate is ten times higher in less equal countries.[23] Portugal's homicide rate is only a little higher than that of egalitarian Finland, and since all these figures come from the 1990s, it can be best explained by poverty, rather than inequality. More recent figures show that Portugal's murder rate has since dropped to around 2 per 100,000 people, similar to that of Sweden.[24]

The USA's high homicide rate is largely driven by black-on-black gun crime and gang activity. The homicide rate for black male victims is 37.59 per 100,000, eight times higher than for white males (4.63 per 100,000).[25] Wilkinson and Pickett could no doubt identify inequality as being the 'root cause' of black-on-black shootings, but the proliferation of handguns, drug wars, poverty and America's unique history are more likely candidates. Whatever the reasons, America is clearly the major outlier in this graph. Figure 4.5 shows the data with the USA excluded. There is plainly no correlation with inequality.

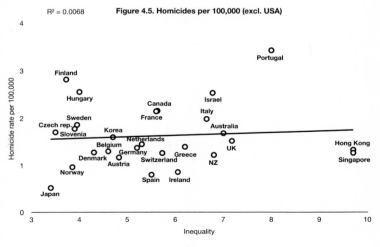

Figure 4.5. Homicides per 100,000 (excl. USA)

It is interesting to note that none of the countries excluded from *The Spirit Level*'s analysis support the inequality-homicide theory. In *The Spirit Level* graph, Finland was the lone outlier amongst the more equal countries, something Wilkinson and Pickett brush off by referring to the high proportion of gun-owners in that country (they do not afford the USA or Israel the same benefit of the doubt). By showing the Czech Republic, Hungary and Slovenia, we can see that Finland is not such an outlier after all. Plenty of 'more equal' societies have an above-average murder rate. Singapore and Hong Kong, on the other hand, have a low murder rate, even lower than more egalitarian South Korea.

Incidentally, the rate for *attempted* murder is four times higher in Sweden than in England and Wales, and eight times higher than in New Zealand.[26] It seems that the emotions that lead people to kill sometimes rage more fiercely in the Nordic soul than in their capitalist counterparts, even if they don't always see it through.

Finally, we must address Wilkinson and Pickett's quirky idea that socialists kill themselves while capitalists kill each other. The graph below shows suicide rates against homicide. If

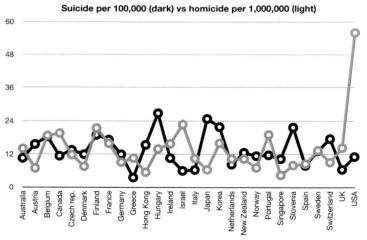

Suicide per 100,000 (dark) vs homicide per 1,000,000 (light)

there was any truth in their theory, we should see a divergence between suicide and homicide.[27] When one goes up the other should go down. The only real examples of this happening are the USA, which, as we have seen, has a very high homicide rate and a fairly low suicide rate, and Japan, which has the opposite. There is no such pattern in the other countries, indeed many of them produce a remarkable degree of symmetry (Belgium, France, Spain, Sweden etc.).

There is a more fundamental reason why Wilkinson and Pickett's theory is wrong. You will notice that the homicide rates are measured in cases per million and suicides are measured in cases per 100,000. Suicides, then, are ten times more common than homicides. If angry people in unequal societies really did direct their anger outwards by killing other people, rather than themselves, the murder rate in these countries would be ten times higher. And that assumes they would only kill one person. Factor in some killing sprees and the rate would be higher still.

In summary, there is no evidence that homicide is inversely related to suicide, nor is there any evidence that egalitarian countries experience less crime, including homicide, than less equal countries.

Infant mortality

5

Infant mortality

"Inequality is associated with higher rates of infant mortality"
— *The Spirit Level* (p. 81)

Infant mortality used to be a sound barometer for overall health in the West. In many countries it still is. Lack of sanitation, poor hygiene, vaccine shortages and infectious diseases continue to kill millions of people in the developing world, with babies at greatest risk. In these countries, infant mortality reflects overall conditions of health, sanitation and medical care.

This is no longer the case in the rich nations that are our focus. Infants dying in the first year of life are now so rare that their numbers tell us little about overall living standards. Consequently, using infant mortality as an indicator of overall health has fallen out of favour in recent years.[1] Rather than being caused by poverty, infant mortality in the West is principally the result of congenital abnormalities, birth defects, premature births and complications during labour. Most of these babies are born critically ill and the relatively rare medical problems that cause their death are almost entirely unrelated to socioeconomic circumstance.

Since genetic defects are not caused by poverty, an association with inequality is highly improbable. It is, however, always easier to find an association than it is to explain it and so, inevitably, a 'link' between inequality and infant mortality has been mooted.

In 1992, shortly after Richard Wilkinson published his first paper on inequality and health in the *British Medical Journal*, a young economist named Robert Waldmann published a study in which he raised the astonishing possibility that an increase in the wealth of the richest 5% leads to an increase in infant mortality amongst the poorest 20%, even when the incomes of the poorest 20% remain unchanged.[2] Wilkinson seized on this as evidence to support his case, and cited it when his ideas came under attack in the 1990s.[3] The association remained inexplicable, however, and in 2009 Waldmann published another paper on the same topic, this time concluding that the apparent correlation was due to expenditure on health care rather than inequality.[4]

Although bereft of any biological explanation, the statistical association between inequality and infant mortality remains tantalising for inequality theorists. Reviewing *The Spirit Level* in the *New Statesman*, Roy Hattersley drew attention to the 'fact' that, when compared to Britain, "only in Portugal, Singapore and the United States of America is life expectancy lower and the infant mortality rate higher."[5]

One wonders how carefully Hattersley read the book for him to make such a blunder. A glance at *The Spirit Level*'s graphs would have told him that several countries, including Denmark, have lower life expectancies than Britain, while both Ireland and New Zealand have higher rates of infant mortality (and Singapore's is much lower). For Hattersley, as with several other reviewers, the remarkable 'link' with infant mortality was evidence of inequality's near-supernatural ability to affect every aspect of life. As with the other aspects, it was a story that was too good to check.

Wilkinson and Pickett's data come from 2000 and they ignore the continued decline in rates since. When the *European*

Perinatal Health Report published figures for 2004, there was very little difference in infant mortality rates across the continent.[6] Portugal, in particular, has seen a dramatic fall in infant mortality despite remaining a very unequal society. A 2006 UNICEF report found that Portugal had reduced its rate from 14 deaths per 1,000 live births in 1990 to fewer than 5 per 1,000 in 2005 (it also noted that this unequal country had the 11th highest life expectancy in the world).[7]

Figure 5.1 shows infant mortality per 1,000 live births. The data come from the United Nations and show average rates from 2000 to 2005.[8] It confirms that income has little effect once countries get to a very high level of development, with the emphasis on *very*. Hungary shows that even small differences in a nation's wealth make an impact. In 1990, the Czech Republic and Slovenia both had rates much higher than that of Hungary today.[9]

The graph below provides extremely modest support for the inequality hypothesis. Firstly, it should be recognised that the variation between countries is very slight. Twenty of the 28 countries fit into a narrow band of 3.9 to 5.2 deaths per 1,000 live births. Once again, most countries do not fit the 'trend'. We

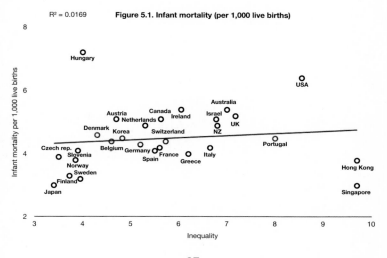

Figure 5.1. Infant mortality (per 1,000 live births)

87

are really talking about differences between Scandinavia, Asia and the USA.

In international terms, the differences between these rich countries are negligible. To put it into context, figure 5.2 shows how the graph looks if we include some other nations. These are by no means the poorest countries in the world. If we were to include countries like Afghanistan or Angola the graph would need to be four times as high.

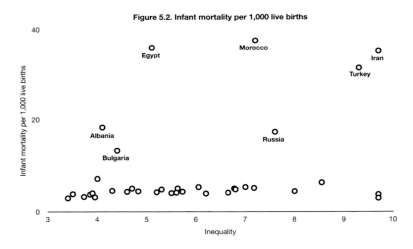

Figure 5.2. Infant mortality per 1,000 live births

Although the differences in infant deaths between the richest countries are relatively small, and vulnerable to year-on-year fluctuations, there is a biological cause. Wilkinson and Pickett's own explanation, that inequality acts like a "pollutant spread throughout society"[10] does not come close to addressing the issue. One can just about imagine resentment at inequality driving someone to murder—people have been doing it since the French Revolution—but is it really plausible that the effects of inequality can be felt *in utero*?

Looking again at Figure 5.1, it is notable that all the countries with the lowest rates are in Scandinavia and Asia, regardless of levels of inequality, while the USA has the highest rate. By comparing rates in Portugal and Slovenia, or Singapore and Japan, we can see that neither inequality nor income have much effect. To understand why the USA has the highest rate of infant mortality, we must first understand the medical reasons for these infants' deaths.

Cot death

If these babies were dying from want, neglect or deprivation, one might be more tempted to point the figure at income inequality or, at least, relative poverty. Perhaps the reader is meant to assume that the principle cause of infant mortality in the West is cot death (or Sudden Infant Death Syndrome). The causes of cot death remain unknown and an avalanche of theories of questionable veracity have attempted to fill the void.

Some of these theories could loosely be described as socioeconomic, as there is an association with the less wealthy, but cot death is only responsible for 5-10% of all infant deaths in developed countries (and far fewer elsewhere). Rates do not vary enough between nations to explain the disparity in overall infant mortality. The lone exception is New Zealand which, for unknown reasons, has long had a peculiarly high rate of cot death.

Premature births

The major cause of infant mortality in nearly all rich countries is preterm (or premature) birth, often combined with low and very low birth-weights. Babies born under the weight of 1,000 grammes account for nearly half of all infant deaths in America, despite representing less than one percent of total births.

86% of extremely low-weight babies (less than 500 grammes) die quickly, often within hours. It is a miracle of scientific advancement that they can be kept alive at all. In earlier times, or in different countries, their deaths would not even be recorded. Indeed, one reason for the USA's apparently high level of infant mortality (relative to other wealthy countries) is that some other nations record infant deaths within the first 24 hours as still-births. In several countries, including the Czech Republic, the Netherlands and France, doctors are not required to report the births of babies born under 500 grammes at all.[11] In the USA, these babies account for 22% of total infant mortality.

Such extreme cases, although rare, have a disproportionate impact on the total mortality figures, but babies born even a few weeks early are three times more likely to die in the first year than babies born after a full term. If the USA had the same number of preterm births as Sweden, it would have an infant mortality rate of 3.9, putting it between Germany and France in our graph.[12]

There are four reasons why preterm births are more common in the USA than in most other countries. Firstly, American doctors have taken to performing caesarean sections in greater numbers in recent years. Almost a third of births involved this procedure in 2005, 50% more than had been the case in the 1990s.[13] Americans also induced twice as many labours than they did in 1991, as Dr Marian F. MacDorman explained:

"Back in the day if a woman had high blood pressure, they might put her in the hospital and wait until the baby is more mature. Now the docs seem more likely to want to delivery the baby early."[14]

Regardless of whether this is a welcome development in midwifery, it accounts for why so many more low weight, preterm babies are being delivered in the USA than in Europe and why, therefore, infant mortality rates have not fallen as quickly. It can scarcely be blamed on inequality. The USA actually has a better record of keeping preterm babies alive than most European countries, but it also delivers many more of them.

Secondly, fertility treatments are used far more often in the USA than elsewhere,[15] leading to a rise in the number of twins, triplets and quadruplets being born. These babies are, of course, much smaller than average. The infant mortality rate for multiple births is six times higher than for single births. The rate for triplets is ten times higher and the rate for quadruplets is eighteen times higher.[16]

Thirdly, the babies of mothers who are in their teens or over the age of 40 are at greater risk of dying within a year, and the risk rises at the most extreme ends of the spectrum (mothers under 16 and those over 45). Teenage births are probably less of a problem in the USA, as their numbers have fallen by a third since 1990, but the number of 40-44 year olds giving birth has risen by around the same amount. In 2003, the USA saw the average age of first-time mothers hit an all time high.[17]

Fourthly, the USA is more racially diverse than any other country studied in *The Spirit Level*. This is one subject which Wilkinson and Pickett prefer not to discuss, but it is well-established that some ethnic groups, particularly blacks, are more likely to give birth before the full term for physiological reasons. Reviewing the evidence for *The Lancet* in 2008, Robert Goldenberg noted that:

In the USA and in the UK, women classified as black, African-American, and Afro-Caribbean are consistently reported to be at higher risk of preterm delivery; preterm rates are in the range of 16-18% in black women compared with 5-9% for white women. Black women are also three to four times more likely to have a very early preterm birth than women from other racial or ethnic groups... East Asian and Hispanic women typically have low preterm birth rates.[18]

Numerous studies have shown disparities in infant mortality rates for different races that cannot be explained by socioeconomic factors.[19] A recent study from Denmark, for example, concluded:

> Among the five largest ethnic minorities, the Turkish, Pakistani and Somali population had substantially higher fetal and infant mortality compared with the Danish majority population, while the Lebanese and Former Yugoslavian minorities were at the same level as the majority population. The excess risk was not attributable to socioeconomic conditions.[20]

In 2005, the infant mortality rate in the USA for black mothers was 13.63 per 1,000 live births, considerably higher than the rate of 5.76 amongst non-Hispanic white mothers, which, in turn, was higher than the rate of 4.89 per 1,000 found amongst Asians and Pacific Islanders.

In Australia, infant mortality rates are two to three times higher amongst Aborigines than amongst whites.[21] In New Zealand, 35% of infant deaths involve Maori mothers, despite Maoris making up only 14% of the population. Maoris also account for 72.5% of cot deaths.[22]

With preterm births three times as common amongst blacks than amongst whites, it should not be surprising that nations with significant black populations have higher rates of infant death than countries like Sweden, which is over 95% caucasian. Although Sweden has a large foreign-born population, its immigrants predominantly come from other Nordic states, the former Yugoslavia, Poland and Iraq. The well-established tendency of East Asians to have few preterm births is the most likely explanation for the very low rate of infant mortality in Japan.

Congenital abnormalities

Preterm birth is the major cause of infant mortality in most developed countries, but not in the USA. There, the biggest single cause—responsible for a fifth of all cases—is congenital abnormality.[23] These abnormalities are, by definition, genetic in origin and, again, there is a clear link with race which cannot be explained by income disparities. Numerous studies have shown that caucasians and East Asians are less likely to give birth to a baby with a congenital abnormality, and that this is not due to underlying socioeconomic circumstances.[24]

Britain's Pakistani community, for example, has been found to have very high infant mortality from congenital abnormalities, a likely result of intermarrying between extended families.[25] The Office for National Statistics reported in 2008:[26]

The figures show that Asian and Black ethnic groups accounted for over 11 per cent of live births in England and Wales in 2005, and 17 per cent of infant deaths.

Babies in the Pakistani and Caribbean groups had particularly high infant mortality rates, 9.6 and 9.8 deaths per 1,000 live births respectively. This was double the rate in the White British group of 4.5 deaths per 1,000 live births.

Half of all infant deaths in the Pakistani group were due to congenital anomalies, compared with only a quarter of deaths in the White British group.

These biological and genetic causes of infant death are not mentioned in *The Spirit Level*. To what extent they explain the disparity in infant mortality rates between countries is not known, but they clearly have the most impact on the USA and the least impact on Asian and Scandinavian countries.

Since the primary causes of infant mortality in the West are largely dictated by genetic defects and physiological characteristics, it is surprising that Wilkinson and Pickett's hypothesis has been received with so little scepticism.

The leading causes of infant mortality in the USA are congenital abnormalities (20%), preterm birth (17%), cot death (8%), maternal complications (6%) and complications with the placenta or cord (4%). All of these are medical problems and only cot death has been associated with income, for reasons which remain unknown. None of them can be convincingly linked to the psychological stress of being less wealthy than one's neighbour. A recent study in *The Lancet* reported that a weak or short cervix was the single most significant predictor of preterm birth.[27] Such medical conditions are not caused by inequality.

A more plausible explanation for the slight disparity in rates of infant mortality can be found in the demographics of each country and in trends in fertility, medical practice and data collection. Even if this analysis overstates the importance of these factors, the low rates of infant mortality in Portugal and Hong Kong, along with the fact that Singapore has the lowest rate in the world*, strongly suggests that inequality does not cause infant death.

* Wilkinson refuses to accept the Singapore figure. At a meeting at the Sheffield Quaker Meeting House in 2008, he said: "I just don't believe the Singapore data. I remember once having to stop in Singapore on a flight to the States. It's the only place where walking along the street in the evening I've been accosted by male and female prostitutes and drug pushers and so on. I do not believe their infant mortality rates are the lowest in the world. If you look at any of their other social problems they are up here where you might expect them to be." (October 31st 2008)

6

Selfish capitalists?

"Just as individuals who trust other people are more likely to give to charity, more equal countries are also more generous to poorer countries."
— *The Spirit Level* (p. 60)

At the heart of Wilkinson and Pickett's thesis is the notion of equal countries fostering an environment in which people become less selfish and more altruistic. One indication of this benevolence, they say, can be seen in the proportion of national income that is spent on foreign aid.

Not surprisingly, just as individuals who trust other people are more likely to give to charity, more equal countries are also more generous to poorer countries.[1]

This public-spirited philanthropy is shown in a graph which does indeed show a marked correlation between equality and foreign aid spending. Figure 6.1 shows government spending on foreign aid as a percentage of national income, using OECD data.[2]

In terms of showing a clear correlation with inequality, this is one of the two strongest graphs in *The Spirit Level*. The other strong graph shows rates of imprisonment (see Chapter 4). It is significant that these are the two criteria where a genuine

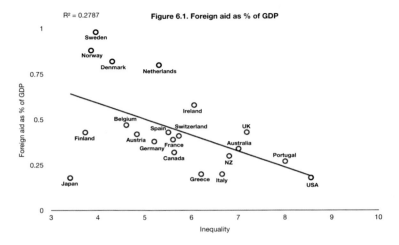

$R^2 = 0.2787$

Figure 6.1. Foreign aid as % of GDP

correlation with inequality can be seen because they are also the two which are directly dictated by government policy. They do not show trends in population behaviour, rather they are a reflection of the type of government that is in charge.

Just as rates of imprisonment do not reflect the crime rate, spending on foreign aid does not reflect the generosity of individuals. It would be more accurate to say that the type of government which prioritises redistribution of wealth is also more likely to spend on foreign aid and is less likely to send criminals to prison.

By focusing solely on government spending, Wilkinson and Pickett are only showing us half the picture. They do not show how much citizens and businesses give to charity. This is an important omission because, as the quote at the beginning of this chapter shows, they lead the reader to believe that people in more equal countries give more to charity. Had they sought out any evidence for this, they would have found the opposite to be true.

Figure 6.2 shows the percentage of GDP voluntarily given to charity by the citizens of ten countries. These figures come

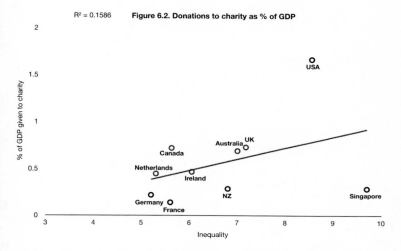

Figure 6.2. Donations to charity as % of GDP

from the Charities Aid Foundation and reflect the trend in 2005, when the most recent data were available.[3] Although not all the countries in our study are included in this analysis, there are enough for us to see a trend towards less equal countries giving more. The only outlier is Singapore, just as Japan is the major outlier in figure 6.1.

This trend is more strongly confirmed in figure 6.3, which shows the average amount each person gave to charity in 2002.[4] Here the correlation is clearer and, again, far from showing themselves to be 'selfish capitalists', Americans are extraordinarily philanthropic. The difference is that they prefer to give privately, rather than via the state, as the journalist Jeffrey Thomas explains:

When it comes to international aid, Americans long have preferred to donate their money through the private sector or to private charities rather than relying on government. The $115.9 billion provided by private foundations, corporations, voluntary organizations, universities, religious organizations and individual Americans in 2007, the most current data available, is more than five times the $21.8 billion of official aid provided by the U.S. government.[5]

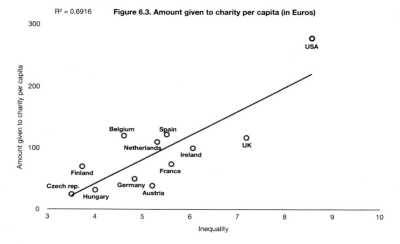

Figure 6.3. Amount given to charity per capita (in Euros)

In 2008, Americans gave $307 billion to charity—2.2% of its gross domestic product—of which more than a third went to the developing world. Even if one excludes donations to religious organisations and schools, the USA gives a larger proportion of its national income to charity than any other country.[6]

The reason for the trends shown in figures 6.2 and 6.3 is not hard to fathom. By taxing people less, countries like the USA leave more money in people's pocket to spend themselves. And by offering tax breaks for those who donate, the US government encourages philanthropy. But in countries where more than half of one's income is immediately appropriated by the state, people feel less obligated to contribute of their own accord and, even if they want to give voluntarily, they have less money left with which to do so. It shouldn't be surprising to find that if the state relieves people of most of their income, they will be less inclined to give away what remains. This is all the more true in countries where citizens are encouraged to believe that the state will take care of everything.

There is, then, a direct *inverse* correlation between higher taxes and charitable giving, as the Charities Aid Foundation states in its report:

Giving tends to represent a lower proportion of GDP in countries with higher levels of personal taxation, particularly social insurance.[7]

Equal and unequal countries donate part of their GDP to good causes in their own way. More egalitarian countries use money from high taxes which is given away as politicians see fit. Low tax countries allow people to give to charities and causes as *they* see fit. But although one system relies on compulsion and the other relies on charity, it is the voluntary system that generates the greatest sums. As shown in figure 3.2, the amount France gives to charity amounts to just 0.14% of GDP, twelve times less than the USA (1.73%). Even if we add the 0.39% France gives in foreign aid it is still a quarter of the American total of 1.91%. When the contribution of individuals is combined with that of the state, it is clear that less equal countries are at least as philanthropic as the rest and often more so.

Recycling

Wilkinson and Pickett also use recycling as a proxy for community-mindedness. They show how much waste is recycled in eleven countries. As you can see in figure 6.4, four of the six most equal countries recycle over 70% of their waste.[8] This, say Wilkinson and Pickett, is proof that there is a "greater sense of public responsibility in more equal countries."[9]

They offer no explanation as to why Germany and Switzerland recycle so much more than France and Spain, nor do they explain the lack of any gradient in this graph. Ignore the linear regression line and you will see two distinct groups; four countries perform well and seven perform poorly. The country that does best of all is Switzerland, which is neither very equal nor very unequal.

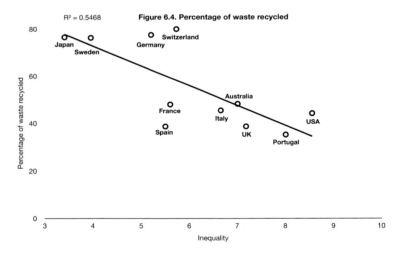

Figure 6.4. Percentage of waste recycled

Once again, if we want to understand why these countries rank as they do, we need to ignore the inequality canard and look at what is going on within them. The explanation for why Japan,

Sweden, Germany and Switzerland recycle twice as much rubbish as the rest is quite simple: compulsion. These countries have the toughest recycling laws in the world. In Japan, for example, anyone disposing of waste needs to abide by the Waste Matter Disposal Law, Amended Recycling Law, Automobile Recycling Law, Food Products Recycling Law, Construction Recycling Law, Household Appliances Recycling Law and the Containers & Packaging Recycling Law. Threatened with stiff penalties for disobedience, the Japanese must separate their household rubbish into twelve categories of recyclables before it is collected.

In Switzerland, where the government has a recycling target of 75%, you have to pay for your household rubbish to be collected and official bin bags cost 5 Swiss francs (£3). Since recycling is free, this offers a very significant incentive to recycle or, as often happens (despite the supposed "greater sense of public responsibility"), dump your rubbish illegally. Those who choose the latter option are well-advised to remove any old bills or letters, as the authorities search through abandoned bin bags and hand out fines of up to 10,000 Swiss francs (£6,000).

Germany and Sweden have similar systems, with minimal refuse collection from the home and mandatory colour-coded recycling stations which must be driven to. Failure to comply results in rubbish being left uncollected and, again, financial penalties. In Sweden, where undercover 'garbage cops' were employed to patrol recycling bays, a 77 year old woman was fined for disposing of a frying pan incorrectly.[10]

The reader may view these measures, which are all largely absent from the other countries in the graph, as reasonable and proportionate. If the intention is to get people to recycle, they are certainly effective. What cannot be argued is that they are the result of more civic-minded people recycling of their own free will. As with foreign aid, the recycling figures reflect government action, not voluntary behaviour.

Ending growth

7

Ending growth

"Society is defined by nothing more and nothing less
than perpetual consumption."
— Neal Lawson, *All Consuming*

Despite its radical hypothesis, *The Spirit Level* was just the latest addition to the library of anti-consumerist literature which blossomed in the first decade of the twenty-first century. Naomi Klein's *No Logo* (2000), Michael Marmot's *Status Syndrome* (2004), Richard Layard's *Happiness* (2005), Oliver James' *Affluenza* and Neal Lawson's *All Consuming* (2010), to name but a few, travelled different routes to come to the same conclusion: economic growth was not the cure, it was the disease.

Each sought, in its own way, a return to a simpler and more 'authentic' way of life, in which material possessions are less important and lives are less stressful; that in the midst of wealth we have lost our soul. It is a timeless theme that has long featured in religion and philosophy. In the second century AD, Tacitus observed that "many who seem to be struggling with adversity are happy; many, amid great affluence, are utterly miserable."

In the eighteenth century, Adam Smith wrote in *The Theory of Moral Sentiments*: "Power and riches... leave [a man] as much, and sometimes more, exposed than before to anxiety, to fear and to sorrow."[1]

Often this money-doesn't-buy-you-happiness sentiment is combined with a wistfulness for a less pampered past. Thomas Carlyle, for example, wrote in 1862:

We have sumptuous garnitures for our life, but have forgotten how to live in the middle of them.[2]

The corrupting influence of advertising was a complaint for later generations, but by the mid-twentieth century this, too, had become a mainstay. The back cover of the revised edition of J.K. Galbraith's *The Affluent Society* asks the question:

Why worship work and productivity if many of the goods we produce are superfluous — artificial 'needs' created by high pressure advertising?

It is with *The Affluent Society* (1958) that the modern anti-consumerist movement began. Reading it now, it is remarkable how little the arguments have evolved in the half-century since. Galbraith argued that capitalist production exceeded demand and that most of the products being manufactured were of negligible utility. Only by aggressively advertising these products could demand be created, and only through a spiral of endless consumerism could the system be maintained. "The more that is produced," wrote Galbraith, "the more that must be owned in order to maintain the appropriate prestige."[3]

People may feel happier after purchasing these new goods but since the forces that drive them to do so are contrived for them, their happiness is invalid. Although they do not realise it, the masses are being driven to buy things they do not truly want. This idea of a manipulated population not acting in its own best interest closely echoes the Marxist notion of 'false consciousness'. The demons that Galbraith identified as the drivers of consumption—status competition and advertising—continue to feature heavily in anti-consumerist tracts today. The solution, he said, was that instead of working harder to buy more useless possessions, the consumer would be better served by having his desires curtailed.

Unless restrained by conventional attitudes, he might wonder if the solution lay with more goods or fewer demons.[4]

These sentiments will be familiar to anyone who has read any anti-consumerist or anti-capitalist book of the last ten years. At its heart is the message that most people have enough and do not need any more. As in *The Spirit Level*, the lesson is that economic growth has taken the West as far as it can and it is time to realign our priorities and redistribute the wealth.

What Wilkinson and Pickett call "our almost neurotic need to shop and consume"[5] has made us forget what is truly important in life. In an interview with the *Boston Globe*, Kate Pickett rejected the notion that people spend for any other reason than to keep up with the Joneses.

"We want bigger houses and more cars, not because we need them, but because we use them to express our status. Material goods are how we show the world we're keeping up, and in a more hierarchical society that's more important. Status competition becomes more intense, and that increases our need to consume."[6]

For Wilkinson and Pickett, it is crucial that the reader becomes convinced that the only consequence of economic growth in the West is a rampant and futile consumerism. If people only spend to compete for status, the products themselves have no intrinsic value and it will be no loss, therefore, if economic growth is brought to a halt and people can buy fewer of them.

Wilkinson and Pickett see themselves standing at the end of an era, beyond which the old ways cannot produce further gains. The fact that Galbraith said much the same thing half a century earlier should give us pause for thought. In 1958, Galbraith cited vacuum cleaners, televisions and wall-to-wall carpets as the unnecessary wants of an affluent society. While none of these are any more essential for survival today than they were fifty years ago, it would take a brave politician to tell the electorate that they would be happier without them.

Galbraith's list of 'unnecessary' products reminds us that things that were once viewed as luxuries are now taken for granted. Further back in history, Adam Smith used linen shirts and leather shoes as examples. These were not, strictly speaking, necessary items and yet since they had become so widely owned, eighteenth century Englishmen were almost expected to wear them. And so, as he wrote in *The Wealth of Nations*, "the established rules of decency" have turned luxuries into necessities.[7]

Smith was not, of course, using this observation as a stick with which to beat capitalism. He saw the fact that yesterday's luxuries become today's essentials as a vindication of the free market system that makes them affordable. But later writers, starting with Galbraith, took the same observation as proof that capitalism produces useless or near-useless products. Today, Smith's linen shirts and Galbraith's vacuum cleaners have been replaced by widescreen televisions and weekend holidays.

The belief that if something is not essential, it cannot be useful, makes a Calvinist virtue of having only the bare necessities. In doing so, it sets capitalism an impossibly high benchmark. Unless a product keeps body and soul together, or produces lasting happiness, it is deemed frivolous, even decadent. The people, meanwhile, are encouraged to set their horizons low. They need little more than food on the table and a roof over their head. So long as everyone has the essentials, no one will suffer materially. So long as no one has much more than the essentials, no one will suffer from the psychosocial traumas of inequality, greed and status anxiety.

Such thinking rests on the fundamental misconception that anything that is not essential has no benefit, except as a status symbol. We do not "need" a bigger house, says Pickett, therefore we desire one only to "express our status". This leap of logic ignores the possibility that a bigger house might be desired because of an expanding family or simply because a more spacious home provides a better standard of living.

It does not take a marketing campaign for us to see that a vacuum cleaner will save us time, nor does it take our neighbour to buy a television for us to see its uses. Just as these products were seen as extravagances in the 1950s, so too were mobile phones, DVDs and broadband in the 1990s. By the rationale of Galbraith and his intellectual descendants, these products have become commonplace as a result of advertising and the race for prestige. An alternative, though hardly obscure, explanation is that they are useful, affordable and an improvement on the products they have replaced. Only by fixating on life expectancy and self-reported happiness can the obvious utility of popular products be overlooked.

The anti-consumerists expect far more from consumer items than those who buy them. For the most part, household goods and consumer durables are purchased to improve one's standard of living, not to attain eternal happiness. How 'happy' these products make us is a moot point. The acquisition of new products tends to provide fleeting happiness insofar as it can be measured. This, say the anti-consumerists, is the killer proof that we are on a carousel of vacuous consumption, endlessly chasing the next transient high while ignoring our fundamental inner needs. Anyone foolish enough to believe that material possessions will provide spiritual fulfillment may find this to be true. We must, however, question how many people really entertain this delusion.

Shopping centres always seem to be full of people, therefore people are always shopping. This is the kind of specious reasoning that inspires the idea that modern society is, as Neal Lawson claims, "defined by nothing more and nothing less than perpetual consumption." Empirical evidence is never presented, but according to a study in the *American Journal of Psychiatry*,

5.8% of the American public are 'compulsive buyers' or 'shopaholics.'[8] In a land of unabashed capitalism, this does not seem to be a sufficiently high percentage to justify Wilkinson and Pickett's claim that "we", as a society, are addicted to "obsessive shopping and spending."[9]

For some people, no doubt, shopping is a leisure activity, even a hobby. For a small minority, retail therapy may even constitute a mild mental disorder. The *American Journal of Psychiatry* study found that those who suffer from depression and generalised anxiety disorder were far more likely to engage in compulsive buying. Oliver James would probably insist that the cause-and-effect works in reverse—that capitalism leads to mental illness, of which compulsive buying is one variety. But, as shown in Chapter 2, depression and generalised anxiety disorder are as common in 'Unselfish Capitalist' countries as they are in 'Selfish Capitalist' countries. It is therefore more plausible to argue that compulsive buying is a symptom of an underlying mental disorder, and a relatively rare one at that.

Elitism

Critics of capitalism no longer tell the public that vacuum cleaners and wall-to-wall carpets are unnecessary wants. It is easier to make the case against the free market if one focuses on diamond-encrusted skulls and designer handbags. High-end purchases and millionaire extravagances feature heavily in anti-consumerist rhetoric because they divert attention from the travelling, entertainment, comfort, good food, health and independence that are the real fruits of economic growth.

In truth, consumer durables make up a small fraction of household expenditure. For the vast majority of us, rent or mortgage repayments take the largest chunk out of the monthly salary, followed by food, clothing and transport. Add in energy bills, insurance and other mundane expenses and it is clear that most income is spent on things that were considered necessities long before globalisation took hold.

The jewellery, plasma televisions and new cars that preoccupy the anti-consumerists are, for all but a privileged few, occasional purchases at best. Their fixation on products that may or may not provide lasting happiness blinds the eye to the money spent on pleasures that we know won't last—restaurants, holidays, wine, cigars, cinema, theatre, *et cetra*. None of these things are necessities, but nor can it be seriously argued that they do not enhance lives or provide pleasure.

If disposable income was being obsessively spent on organic food and French cinema, one suspects the anti-consumerists might find economic growth more tolerable. The resentment comes not from the affluence *per se*, but from what the money is being spent on. And that is good old fashioned snobbery.

Ironically, the anti-consumerists are not averse to rampant consumerism in their own lives. *Affluenza* begins with Oliver James recalling his fury when his publisher offered him what he considered to be a derisory advance for his book. He needed the money, he explains, for a new computer, a new mobile phone, a DVD player for his toddler and, despite his deep concern over rising levels of carbon dioxide, a series of long-haul flights.

Neal Lawson's *All Consuming*—an anti-shopping polemic which attempts to exploit the 2009 recession to turn the reader against the free market—begins with the author describing his typical morning. He is woken by his BlackBerry Pearl mobile phone, rises from his Habitat bed, steps onto his John Lewis carpet, wraps himself in a White Company towel, *et cetera*.

The purpose of all this navel-gazing is, presumably, to show that even highly enlightened individuals are not immune from the disease of consumerism. In fact, what are supposed to be endearing admissions of weakness sound more like the hypocrisy of champagne socialists. The sweeping, metropolitan generalisations and the 'we're all in the same boat' assumptions soon become grating. Rather oddly for a former advisor to

Gordon Brown, Neal Lawson views the last years of the previous Conservative government with nostalgia.

[In 1996] I don't recall thinking I've bought sixteen shirts but I really need thirty-two. I seem to remember having enough. And it's funny but I don't remember making any conscious decision to buy twice as many shoes, socks or pants in the intervening years. Somehow it just happened. I graduated from five pairs of shoes to ten, from three weekend breaks a year to six, from a meal out once a week to twice — all without a thought or care. Does that sounds familiar?

For the vast majority of British people, the answer to that question will be a bewildered 'No'. And if you are still wondering what a White Company towel is, you, like me, will be one of them.

As regards holidays, according to Lawson, "we" see Cuba as "'so last year'" and "we" are now travelling to Venezuela and Mongolia instead. Neither Lawson nor James show any sign of being aware quite how elitist they sound. Occasional sneering references to cheap flights for the masses (thereby forcing people like Lawson to travel to increasingly remote destinations to avoid them) betray this implicit snobbery. It is not wealth, but wealth in the wrong hands that is really being objected to.

Lawson explicitly blames the post-war boom for this:

By the 1950s, for the first time in our history, we were producing enough to allow choice for the masses.[10]

Despite their support for some degree of socialist planning, anti-consumerists tend to be culturally conservative. Their utopias rarely differ greatly from the country of their youth. Lord Sainsbury and the Queen of England are not the villains of these books. It is the conspicuous consumption of working class millionaires like the Beckhams and Alan Sugar that is seen as symptomatic of societal malaise. Those with old money would never display their wealth so ostentatiously.

Worse still, those with new money convince other people from humble backgrounds that they can do it too. Oliver James looks back fondly on the days when people knew their place and deference held sway:

Whereas in 1950 poor people regarded the rich and famous as remote figures who had nothing to do with them, now the press and, above all, television, make these people's lifestyles visibly accessible, and modern values encourage them to believe that they too could be rich.[11]

Elsewhere in *Affluenza*, James complains that "everyone is told they can be rich if they work hard enough"[12] as if it would be better to accept that one will die as one was born, either very rich or very poor. This, after all, was the situation in the class-ridden hierarchies that predated capitalism, and remains so in much of the world.

Nostalgia for Britain's immediate post-war years would be puzzling to anyone who lived through those times. Shortages were endemic while the black market thrived. Rationing of meat, eggs, bread, poultry, petrol and bacon continued for years after the war. As David Kynaston concluded in *Austerity Britain*:

Few adults who had to live through the 1940s would readily forgo the prospect of a little more ease, a little more comfort.[13]

And yet the era of powdered eggs and endless queueing has an uncanny hold over some on the left* who see it, with some justification, as the high watermark of big government. It might have been a thoroughly miserable time to be alive, but at least the misery was equally distributed. Better still, post-war privations gave the state unprecedented control over the population through rationing while the rich were stung with luxury taxes.

* Closely followed by the dreary 1970s and, for Wilkinson and Pickett at least, the "highly egalitarian" hunter-gatherer societies of prehistory.

This rose-tinted view of the 1940s rests on some dubious assumptions. It is true that inequality was reduced somewhat as a result of rationing and full employment. Wilkinson and Pickett claim that this led to "camaraderie and social cohesion" which, in turn, led to better health and less crime. For his part, Layard says that "the only situation where we might willingly accept a pay cut is when others are doing the same. That is why there was so little economic discontent during the Second World War."[14]

Leaving aside the question of whether social cohesion really can, by itself, prevent ill-health, it is surely more likely that wartime "camaraderie" was a result of fighting for national survival while being bombed by the Luftwaffe, rather than the modest reduction in income inequality. The threat of invasion is also a better explanation for the lack of "economic discontent" than universal pay cuts. Indeed, once the war was over, it was only a few months before the dockers went on strike. And as for the drop in crime, a far more plausible explanation is the conscription and export of several million young men.

For the revisionists, the war itself was incidental to the emergency policies which accompanied it. Wilkinson and Pickett look back fondly on rationing and luxury taxes as "egalitarian policies implemented... to gain public co-operation in the war effort", as if the goal was to redistribute wealth rather than to save scarce resources. They cite global warming as the new emergency but *The Spirit Level* is not, of course, a book about environmentalism and, from their point of view, the true benefit of carbon quotas is that "income would be redistributed from the rich to poor."[15]

Also citing climate change as a justification for big government, Neal Lawson concludes that "there really is no option" but to introduce rationing for food, air travel and domestic heating.[16] A luxury tax is also needed, he says, offering the questionable but familiar explanation that "no one gets any happier through the accumulation of more and more expensive items."[17]

The system of 'tradeable carbon quotas' espoused by Wilkinson and Pickett is, of course, rationing in all but name. Since carbon dioxide is a by-product of almost everything that is bought and sold, this form of rationing would be more far-reaching than anything implemented during the Second World War. Wilkinson and Pickett's "electronic card to cover payments for fuel, power and air travel"[18] would be the modern-day equivalent of a ration book. It could even incorporate that other war-time invention, the identity card.

There is, of course, a fundamental difference between rationing in war-time and rationing in an age of plenty. In the 1940s, reducing people to the bare essentials was seen as an unfortunate but inevitable consequence of limited means. The case for rationing today is made the other way round: resources are too plentiful and rationing is unfortunate, but it will have the beneficial effect of reducing people to the bare essentials.[19]

In 2009, having squared this circle, the left-wing New Economics Foundation began its Ration Me Up campaign. As part of what it called 'The Great Transition', the group handed out replica Second World War ration books which set limits for much more than bacon and eggs. Andy Wimbush, the NEF's Communications Assistant, explained:

Flicking through the book, I find coupons for almost every activity in my life: taking a bath, running a fridge, eating vegetables, boiling a kettle, taking a bus, even buying a pair of socks. On the back of the book is a grid of forty squares. These forty squares, I'm told, represent my carbon ration for one month.[20]

Though gimmicky, these ration books were designed to be used by the willing and to act as a guide to the future for the unwilling. As the NEF campaign explained:

We recommend that you become accustomed to its content and tasks associated with calculating your monthly carbon usage. For it may well be that in the future, if we do stand true to our country's commitment of reducing our carbon emissions by 80% by 2050, such rationing will be enforced.[21]

Few things highlight the warped priorities of the left in the noughties better than this yearning for generalised poverty. As Britain drifted towards recession from the end of 2007, several newspaper columnists celebrated what they hoped would be a baptism of austerity.

"I hope that the recession now being forecast by some economists materialises," wrote George Monbiot in *The Guardian* under the headline 'Bring on the recession'. Like Wilkinson and Pickett, he believed that economic growth had done its work and must now be curtailed:

Is it not time to recognise that we have reached the promised land, and should seek to stay there? Why would we want to leave this place in order to explore the blackened wastes of consumer frenzy followed by ecological collapse? Surely the rational policy for the governments of the rich world is now to keep growth rates as close to zero as possible?[22]

This pining for austerity was not limited to climate change evangelists like Monbiot. Spoilt by years of affluence, newspaper pundits had either forgotten or did not care that reversing economic growth meant a permanent state of recession.

In August 2008, *The Independent* published a column by Tim Lott titled, with no trace of irony, 'Bring on the pain of the recession and purge our coarsened souls'. The recession, he predicted, would be a blessing in disguise. Unhappily married couples would not be able to afford to divorce, youth unemployment would lead to a "creative upsurge" (presumably in blues music) and small shops on the high street would thrive as the journey to out-of-town shopping centres became too expensive.

But for Lott, the greatest benefit would be in curtailing the "moral rot" of consumerism.

After all there is no doubt that the past 10 years has (sic) seen a exponential increase in vulgarity, greed and stupidity. And, of course, shopping, which encompasses all three.[23]

A week later, in *The Sunday Times*, India Knight announced that "I am happy to observe that the decades of vulgar excess are finally over." In an article titled 'Aah, what a relief the boom has turned to bust', she marvelled at the way we used to live.[24] Since the way "we" used to live included "weekend pads in the country" and "buying handbags that cost the upper end of three figures," Knight was speaking less for Britain than for its metropolitan elite. And how easy it was for newspaper columnists with safe jobs to romanticise the hardship of recession, just as it was easy for the affluent Oliver James and Baron Layard of Highgate to tell the masses that they would be happier with less.

When the full impact of the recession hit home a few months later, these columnists had the good sense to shut up about unemployment cleansing the soul for fear of being lynched by their readers. By the time *The Spirit Level* appeared on the shelves in March 2009, Britain was well into the longest recession since the 1930s. The anti-consumerists no longer had to fantasise about what a world without economic growth would look like.

Ending growth

8

The Great Transition

"Democracy aims at equality in liberty.
Socialism desires equality in constraint and in servitude."
- Alexis De Tocqueville

Writing in 1958, J.K. Galbraith wondered why "inequality has ceased to preoccupy men's minds."[1] He was puzzled by how an issue that had once been so prominent in American politics had slipped down the agenda. Part of the reason, he said, was that working men did not compare themselves to the super-rich, but to one another.

Envy almost certainly operates efficiently only as regards near neighbours. It's not directed towards the distant rich.[2]

The new breed of anti-consumerists explicitly reject this thinking. According to Wilkinson and Pickett:

By comparison with the rich and famous, the rest of us appear second-rate and inferior... the consumption of the rich reduces everyone's satisfaction with what they have.[3]

Oliver James blames this on television:

Once, we used to keep up with the Joneses who lived in our street. Now, thanks largely to TV, it's the Beckhams.[4]

But is it really true that we try to "keep up" with a footballer who reputedly earns a million dollars a week? It would be a soul-crushingly futile experience if we did, and perhaps the former England captain and his wife are given too much prominence in the anti-consumerists' view of the world. The Beckhams' lifestyle holds an uncanny fascination for many, to be sure, but their wealth is so vast that it is doubtful whether people regard them any differently than previous generations viewed Aristotle Onassis or J.D. Rockefeller. We may be interested in them as individuals, but if we compare ourselves with anybody, it is with those we know. In that sense, things have not changed greatly since 1950. The super-rich are still considered a class apart.

It is an ongoing source of frustration to the left that the public do not share their resentment of multi-millionaires. When Tony Blair said, in 2001, "It is not a burning ambition for me to make sure that David Beckham earns less money," he enraged those who purport to speak for the working class.[5] This rage was, however, seldom echoed by the working class themselves. The reason for this was, again, identified by Galbraith in *The Affluent Society*. As long as the free market continues to generate wealth for all, they have no reason to demand its destruction.

The individual whose own income is going up has no real reason to incur the opprobrium of this discussion. Why should he identify himself, even remotely, with soapbox orators, malcontents, agitators, communists, and other undesirables?[6]

Galbraith understood that economic growth pours water on the fire of socialism. As long as everybody's living standards are rising, complaining about inequality looks like straightforward envy. Today, as in 1958, inequality preoccupies middle-class intellectuals rather more than it does the man in the street. In *Status Syndrome*, Michael Marmot discusses the stubborn refusal of ordinary Americans to become less happy even as their country becomes less equal. The second sentence is perhaps the most telling in the entire book:

Changes in income inequality did not affect happiness levels of the poor. The subgroup of the population whose happiness declined when income inequality increased, were richer people who described themselves as on the left politically.[7]

Working class indifference to inequality, so long as their own circumstances are improving, is seen as another example of false consciousness by those who are 'on the left politically'. In *What's Left?*, Nick Cohen describes how socialists came to feel betrayed by the very people they purported to help. The seeds of divorce were sown when millions of workers deserted them in the 1980s in favour of Conservative and Republican brands of individualism, patriotism and free market economics.

Margaret Thatcher and Ronald Reagan won repeatedly because large numbers of voters from the skilled working class supported them. They were never forgiven for that because from their different points of view Fabians, liberals and Marxists had hoped the working class would take power under their leadership. When it didn't, they despised the working class for its weakness and treachery and condemned its members for their greed and obsession with celebrity.[8]

With greater wealth came greater independence. Decades of affluence, rising wages and home-ownership made the working class less reliant on paternal socialism and the labour movement. Today, the left seldom refer to the working class directly, preferring instead to talk about the 'deprived', a term which usefully implies theft. And by 'deprived' they principally mean people on benefits, of whom there are six million in Britain alone, and whose reliance on the state is absolute.

The brand of authoritarian socialism espoused in such books as *The Spirit Level* is fundamentally different from traditional socialism. The left of old desired to increase the workers' wages and improve their living standards. Planned economies, they said, were not just fairer but were more efficient. A Marxist system was capable of producing greater economic growth than capitalism.

Seventy years of communism made a mockery of that assertion. By 1990, few doubted that the free market was the most effective way of increasing national income and raising living standards. With that battle lost, some on the left have attempted to turn capitalism's greatest strength into a weakness. A view has emerged of affluence as a problem in itself, of living standards being good enough and often *too* good. Since working (and even non-working) men and women are no longer materially deprived, there is no need to give them more money (which, goes the thinking, they would only squander on handbags and knick-knacks anyway).

The primary objective of the new left is not to raise income or improve material conditions but to curtail and control consumption. Taxation has become a means in itself. Whether it is taken at source as income tax, or taken at the checkout as sales tax, taxation limits the consumption that destroys the planet and diminishes the soul.

By no means are their sights aimed only at the super-rich. In *The Spirit Level*, Portugal is included as one of the countries that is already rich enough and requires no further growth, despite having a per capita GDP that is less than half of the USA's. In *The Selfish Capitalist*, we are told that our "basic material needs" are met with an income of £15,000 a year and that once that level has been reached, people become "highly materialistic."[9]* Since the median British wage was £23,200 at

---

* Layard says that above $20,000 (roughly £15,000) per person "higher average income is no guarantee of greater happiness." (*Happiness*, p. 34)

the time, this meant that most working people already had too much.[10]

How the government spends the resulting tax revenue is less important than preventing the feckless public from spending it in the first place. As with rationing, what was once seen as an unfortunate side effect—people having less—becomes the intended consequence. Since the public has proven incapable of spending the spoils of growth in a satisfactory manner, growth should be curtailed and the public should hand over its disposable income to those who would spend it more wisely.

Lawson calls this "democratic paternalism" and states that "governments should be empowered to act to force us to stop consuming."[11] Wilkinson and Pickett complain that "the strength of our consumerist tendencies has reduced government to a state of paralysis."[12] James says that "one of the choices we make as voters is to bestow power on our rulers to control our behaviour."[13] All of them display a fundamental misunderstanding of who is supposed to be serving whom in a democracy. But, fortuitously for them, relieving people of their money is one thing that governments do reasonably competently.

Taxing us to happiness

Whether they begin by discussing equality (*The Spirit Level*), mental health (*Affluenza*), shopping (*All Consuming*), health (*Status Syndrome*) or quality of life (*Happiness*), all anti-consumerist tracts end with a call to arms involving higher taxes, bigger government and fresh prohibitions. The route can sometimes be circuitous but the destination is always the same.

Perhaps the most extraordinary idea put forward in *Happiness* is Layard's claim that wealth is a negative externality that should be taxed as if it were literally a pollutant. This rests on the Galbraithian belief that people do not materially benefit from earning more than $20,000 a year, therefore the only reason people want more money is for the psychological benefit of having more than others. But by earning more, they reduce the happiness of others and make *them* work harder to catch up.

So begins a sort of arms race, with everyone working harder and harder to raise their income for no other reason than to leapfrog others. No one ever really benefits because, as Layard sees it, happiness is a zero-sum game; as one person moves up the ladder, someone else must move down. The communal pot of happiness never gets bigger, we all just wind up working harder.

The ideal solution to this arms race would be unilateral disarmament, but since not everyone will agree to this, the state must intervene. Taxes, says Layard, "make it possible to charge people for the damage which they do to others—and so force them to take this damage into account."[14] In addition to compensating society for this psychological 'pollution', a punitive tax system would, Layard says, also restore the work-life balance of which he is so fond.

Taxes discourage us from overwork, from running on a treadmill that brings less advance in happiness than we expected.[15]

Put like that, it is almost as if the government would be doing us a favour by relieving us of the fruits of our labour. Such a system would, however, leave the government as the sole arbiter of what constitutes a correct work-life balance and, indeed, what constitutes happiness.

If Layard's pollution theory sounds like tortured logic, it is in keeping with his other justification for raising taxes, which takes its inspiration from tobacco. Again using his beloved happiness surveys as evidence, Layard quite reasonably suggests that self-reported happiness does not rise in line with living standards because we soon become accustomed to a better standard of living. For a brief period we enjoy our extra comfort and convenience but we soon get used to it and look for other pleasures. This, Layard concludes rather tenuously, means that higher living standards are like a drug. We need more and more of them to satisfy us.

Still more tenuously, Layard equates higher living standards with cigarettes. If we knew that the quest for a higher standard of living was addictive, we would never have started. And what do governments do with cigarettes? They tax them heavily. *Quod erat demonstrandum*, the state must use taxes to stop us consuming.

This mind-boggling combination of rhetorical tricks and *non sequiturs* suggests an unfulfilled career as a defence lawyer. Ingenious though they are, Layard's theories rely on assumptions that are suspect when not plain wrong. He assumes, for instance, that there is no inherent value in raising living standards beyond the fleeting pleasure one enjoys from the novelty of improved circumstance. By this logic, the benefit of moving into a more spacious house is lost once the owner becomes accustomed to his new surroundings. Layard represents the desire for further improvement as proof that all previous goals led to broken dreams and that any pleasure that doesn't result in permanent bliss is a worthless addiction.

Citing the fact that the proportion of people describing themselves as 'very happy' has barely changed since the 1960s, Layard claims this as proof that affluence does not make people happier. In doing so, he exhibits the fixation with money that afflicts all anti-consumerists. A more obvious interpretation of a graph that shows flat-lining happiness for 50 years would be that *nothing* makes us happier. Recessions come and go. Wars are fought. Governments go in and out of office. Crime and unemployment rises and falls. The rise of home-ownership, the creation of the NHS, the golden age of pop music, the invention of the internet—none of this seems to affect our 'happiness'. But since none of the technological, cultural, political or economic events of the last fifty years have had any success in increasing self-reported happiness, the idea that raising taxes and limiting living standards will suddenly yield returns must be regarded as wildly improbable.

At least he does not compare the free market to Stalinism. The same cannot be said for Neal Lawson who plunges new depths of relativism in *All Consuming*:[16]

Totalitarianism, the accusation levelled against Communism, is a system of control that regulates every aspect of public and private life. Consumerism and Communism are two different versions of totalitarianism societies: both offer a pseudo-vision of freedom but operate to systematically refine their dominance.

Having rendered the reader dumbstruck with this stupefying comparison between the richest and healthiest societies that have ever been and spirit-crushing dictatorships that starved and murdered tens of millions of their own citizens,* Lawson sets out his own "pseudo-vision of freedom". Borrowing rather more heavily from totalitarian Communism than from 'totalitarian Consumerism', this vision involves a tax on all advertising, taxes on 'luxuries', warning labels on SUVs ('This car will damage everyone's health'), a Soviet-style citizen's wage and the rationing of food and fuel.

Lawson's representation of 'totalitarian Consumerism' as a living entity which seeks to "systematically refine [its] dominance" implies that the free market is a conscious being capable of thought and intent; as if Adam Smith's invisible hand had an invisible mind and body attached. This echoes Oliver James' idea of capitalism (or rather Affluenza) as a physical virus. Like *Happiness* and, to some extent *All Consuming*, *Affluenza* reads like a self-help book for materialists until one reaches the final third.

Although embellished over 500 pages, the message of *Affluenza* can be boiled down to 'work less and spend more time

---

* An equal opportunities offender, Lawson also equates the free market with the Nazis. Quoting Alan Milburn saying "whether we like it or not, this is a consumer age", Lawson urges to reader to imagine Winston Churchill saying "whether we like it or not, this is a fascist age."

with friends and family.' These are the quite natural sentiments of a well-to-do professional who has recently turned 50 and become a father for the first time; two events that are invariably more interesting to experience than to read about. *Affluenza* offers perfectly sound advice for those who need it: don't borrow more than you can afford to pay; find a job you enjoy; don't work if you don't have to; don't be vain; don't watch too much television, and so forth.

The wheels only really come off when James attempts to weld homespun philosophy to political solutions. Some of these, such as introducing a maximum wage and banning the use of "exceptionally attractive models" in advertising (who will be the judge?), are standard fare amongst the left. Others, such as tightening up inheritance tax and killing off private education, pose no threat to Oliver James now that his Eton days are long behind him and his parents are dead.

His other ideas are so idiosyncratic and impractical that they can only be judged as a response to James' own preoccupations. One can almost hear his infant screaming in the background as he calls for MPs to be forced to look after a two-year old for a fortnight and for parents to be paid the average national wage for the first three years of a child's life. His fixation with property* manifests itself in the bizarre idea of having the government value every house in the country and then "knock a nought off", a ruse that would plunge every mortgage-holder in the UK into negative equity. Finally, his loathing of the USA manifests itself in his demand that American TV shows be limited to one per channel per day, and the operation of American companies in Britain be restricted.

By the time James had followed up his best-seller with *The Selfish Capitalist* in 2008, he was showing signs of having dwelt on his obsessions for too long. Selfish Capitalism had ceased to

---

* James spends seven pages discussing his recurring property-related dreams (*Affluenza*, p. 214-220)

be a catchy phrase and was now a living, breathing organism that was not just responsible for the world's ills but had deliberately and maliciously set out to create them. Selfish Capitalism, he claimed, encourages teen births because the "children's consumer goods market is now worth £30 billion."[17] It seeks to destroy family life because the family "poses an authentic alternative to workaholia."[18] It discourages nationalism because nationalism "creates barriers to corporate globalisation" and it welcomes crime waves because the insurance industry "gains more from policyholder payments than it loses for theft."

In the final chapter, James enters tin-foil hat territory, describing the general public as "happy clappy consumerists—obsessed, unquestioning dupes of corporations and politicians." After applauding the work of Michael Moore, Noam Chomsky, Hugo Chavez and Fidel Castro,[19] it is with a certain inevitability that he puts his weight behind 9/11 conspiracy theories[20] and suggests that failed terrorist attacks in Britain were "sabotaged by the British agents who had then allowed the attacks to go ahead, or even, mounted by terrorists who had actually been encouraged by British agents."[21]

So much for psychologists. What about the epidemiologists? If the reader hasn't realised that *The Spirit Level* is a deeply political book by the time he gets to the final chapter, he can be under no illusion once the authors declare that "it falls to our generation, to make one of the biggest transformations in human history." Like James, Layard and Lawson, Wilkinson & Pickett support a higher top rate of tax, carbon rationing and a maximum wage. The book is short on details but their website (www.equalitytrust.org.uk) finds them calling for "more progressive income and property taxes and more generous benefits" as well as "increasing the bargaining power of trade unions."[22]

These redistributive, tax-and-spend policies hardly represent a radical departure for the left. Galbraith concluded *The Affluent Society* with a similar plea for higher taxes and more generous benefits (although he admitted the latter would result in more "malingering"). Wilkinson and Pickett's only reservation is that such policies do not go far enough. Their fear is that the existing political system will allow socialist reforms to be overturned in the future:

> ...even if effective tax changes were devised and introduced, a new government with different political allegiances could simply reverse them all.[23]

The objective, then, must be to reshape nations in a way that no democratically elected government can undo.

> ...we need to find ways of ensuring that greater equality is more deeply rooted in the fabric of our society and less vulnerable to the whim of successive governments. We need to address the concentrations of power at the heart of economic life.[24]

Wilkinson and Pickett shy away from spelling out how this is to be achieved. They offer just two suggestions, both of which fit the old Marxist notion of 'seizing the means of production'.

One of these is to radically change the world's copyright and patent laws. Not an obvious place for the battle against inequality to begin, but interesting nonetheless. It does, at least, address a genuine problem. The internet has put an enormous strain on copyright and, unless a technological solution can be found, this looks set to continue. In a few years time, the music industry will probably not exist as we know it today. Film, literature, games and computer software are all under threat from file-sharing. Although some people argue that the concept of intellectual property is meaningless and anachronistic, it is hard to deny that if movie makers receive no money for their efforts, there will be no movies. It is, then, a real issue and Wilkinson and Pickett have a predictable solution: more big government.

Wilkinson and Pickett suggest that governments negotiate to buy the rights for music, films, software, inventions, drug patents and scientific journals, and then allow the public free access. This is 'free' in the sense of it being paid for with taxpayers' money, but it would guarantee that studios, artists and researchers (including, of course, epidemiologists) get paid for work that might otherwise be accessed illegally.

It would also put the state in charge of whole sections of the economy that are currently in private ownership. This is why Wilkinson and Pickett find the idea so appealing. The state would control the means of production in the digital age. The effect would be that the government gets to decide which films are made, which books get published, which record companies receive funding and what research gets commissioned.

Put bluntly, and with only slightly excessive cynicism, this would put the job of discovering the next Bob Dylan or Michel Houellebecq in the hands of the people who created the Millennium Dome. If this policy was extended to newspapers—who have suffered from the digital revolution as much as anyone—it would seriously compromise the freedom of the press. Wilkinson and Pickett do not linger on the implications of all this in *The Spirit Level*, but speaking at Birkbank College, London in 2009, Wilkinson was less guarded:

"The internet and digitisation potentially offer the possibility of providing a huge new area of public goods. All entertainment, all the written word, all computer programs and games. All music. All these things can now be made available virtually free to the population of the world. That's a huge socialist opportunity."[25]

Wilkinson and Pickett's other idea is to 'encourage' employee-owned businesses. They cite a number of studies showing increased productivity and happier staff in companies which are owned and run as co-operatives. Good news if true, but, if so, these firms need no encouragement from the government to prosper. They do not require "additional incentives" nor is there any reason for the taxpayer to subsidise them. If employee-owned companies are genuinely more efficient, then eventually all businesses will be run that way. If they are better employers, staff will be lining up to work for them and, as ever in the free market, other companies will have to adapt or die.

That's capitalism. And under capitalism, individuals, families or friends are free to set up and run their business as they see fit, sharing executive power and distributing the profits in whichever way they feel is fair. They can form a commune if they want. They can even refuse to trade with those who do not share their political beliefs. It is not the capitalist, but the socialist, who compels others to live by his rules. And while he believes his egalitarian utopia to be manifestly superior to that of the existing order, it is the socialist who requires compulsion to implement it. And there can be no doubt that fulfilling Wilkinson and Pickett's stated aim of having 100% of businesses employee-run will require compulsion barely hinted at by their coy suggestion that "companies might be required to transfer a proportion of shares each year."[26]

These two recommendations aside, Wilkinson and Pickett refuse to offer a manifesto for how the great 'transformation' is to come about. Their mission for now, they say, is to plant seeds.

At this stage, creating the political will to make society more equal is more important than pinning our colours to a particular set of policies to reduce inequality.[27]

One reason for this skittishness is their desire to convince the reader that large-scale wealth redistribution is not the only route to equality. This is a point that is hammered home time and time again in *The Spirit Level*:

"...there are many different ways of reaching the same destination." (p. 236)

"...there are quite different roads to the greater equality which improves health and reduces social problems (p. 237)

"...there are two quite different paths to greater equality" (p. 238)

"...there are many ways of diminishing inequality" (p. 238)

"...the argument for greater equality is not necessarily the same as the argument for big government." (p. 238)

This is disingenuous. The only country in their study that achieved greater equality without high taxes is Japan and, as so often in *The Spirit Level*, Japan is an exceptional case. As Wilkinson and Pickett admit, Japan's wealth gap was reduced partly as a result of its establishment being crippled by defeat in the Second World War. More significantly, wages have been kept high across all social classes as a result of fewer women being in the workplace (Japan comes well below other rich countries in the gender equality league table).[28]

Since there is no prospect of the clock being turned back for Western women in the workplace, the Japanese experience is unlikely to be replicated. For the countries that are our focus, the only way to become 'more equal' is to raise taxes significantly. Figure 8.1 shows the correlation between taxation (as a proportion of GDP) and inequality.[29] For the reasons given above, Japan and Korea are outliers. All the other countries show

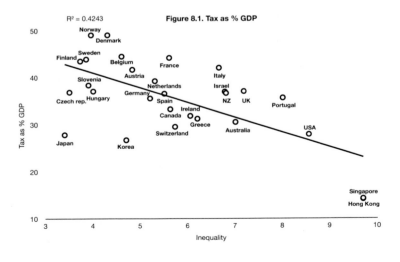

Figure 8.1. Tax as % GDP

a clear pattern, with the Nordic states taking nearly twice as much tax as the USA and more than three times as much tax as Singapore and Hong Kong. The correlation remains strong even if the Asian countries are excluded.

This is the elephant in the room throughout *The Spirit Level*. When the authors talk about 'more equal' countries, what they really mean is high tax countries. Replicating the Scandinavian model would require the state to take half of GDP. If wealth is to be transfered from the individual to the government on such a scale, we are entitled to ask what we will be getting in return. The answer, as we have seen, is not a lot.

The Spirit Level fallacy

9

The Spirit Level fallacy

> "Statistics are like bikinis.
> What they reveal is suggestive, but what they conceal is vital."
> - Aaron Levenstein

This book began by talking about Hollywood actors. You may recall the study that showed Oscar winners living four years longer than unsuccessful nominees. This was reported by the BBC, CBS, ABC, Sky, the *Washington Post* and *The Telegraph* as scientific proof that inequality and low status affects the health and well-being of even the most affluent people. Richard Layard mentions the study twice in *Happiness*. Michael Marmot, in *Status Syndrome*, cites it as compelling evidence that status influences health, and the finding is put top and centre of the book's back cover:

Why do Oscar Winners live for an average of four years longer than other Hollywood actors?

Nevertheless, the 'Oscar winners live longer' story is not true. In 2006, five years after publishing it, *Annals of Internal Medicine* issued a reanalysis of the data and found that the original study had suffered from 'immortal time bias'.[1] Epidemiologists have known about immortal time bias, or 'survival selection treatment bias', since the nineteenth century. An example would be the observation that Popes live longer than artists, from which you might deduce that artists live unhealthier lifestyles and are more prone to disease.[2]

Even if your assumption about their relative lifestyles is correct, you would be wrong about their longevity. Popes do not live longer than artists, they just live long enough to become Pope.[3]

So it is with Oscar winners. They have to fulfill one criterion—they must live long enough to receive the award. In the case of Jessica Tandy and George Burns, that meant living to the age of 79 and 80 respectively. The actors who never won an Oscar had no criteria to fulfill, they could die at any time and still be counted in the *Annals of Internal Medicine* study. There was, therefore, an inherent bias at work. That was the reason Oscar winners appeared to live longer.

The 2006 study reanalysed the data, taking care to avoid immortal time bias. When this was done, there was no statistically significant difference between the longevity of those who won Oscars and those who did not. This reanalysis received a fraction of the international publicity that had accompanied the more sensational findings of the original, but the editors of the journal published an addendum saying "we urge everyone to observe much greater caution about claiming the existence of an 'Oscar effect' on life span." The authors of the new study simply concluded:

Of course, readers and commentators should be doubly cautious whenever they encounter statistical results that seem too extreme to be true.

The reader might exercise similar caution with regards to *The Spirit Level* and its attempts to apply the lessons of the Oscar study to whole societies. Much has been made of *The Spirit Level*'s credentials as a piece of scientific research. "It demonstrates," wrote Roy Hattersley, "the scientific truth of the assertion that social democrats have made for a hundred years."[4]

Wilkinson and Pickett are both epidemiologists by profession and *The Spirit Level* uses the statistical methods of epidemiology throughout. Many of these methods were developed by the botanist and statistician Ronald Aylmer Fisher in the 1920s for the purpose of studying plants.[5] He would, for example, grow two groups of tomato plants under near-identical conditions, one with and the other without the application of fertilizer, then compare rates of growth, attributing the difference to the effect of the single deviating condition, i.e. the fertilizer.

The strength of such experiments lay in the researcher's ability to randomise the samples and control the conditions. Since the only difference between the two samples was the external element (in this example, fertiliser), any difference between the two could be attributed, with a high level of probability, to that external element. When applied to humans, the randomised control trial becomes more problematic. Humans and human disease vectors are more complex than are tomato plants and fertilizers, so what were reasonably reliable statistical techniques when applied to tomatoes become potentially misleading with regard to the causation of disease in a human population.

In some experiments, these problems can be minimised through the use of the double-blind trial and by choosing subjects who are similar in terms of age, diet, gender, race and lifestyle. Although groups of humans will never be identical in the way that a set of tomato seeds or plants are identical, every effort is taken to make them at least comparable.

But when entire nations are studied, these problems become virtually insurmountable. Comparing aggregate data from whole countries is as far from the randomised controlled double-blind trial as it is possible to get under the mantle of science. Neither random nor controlled, ecological studies (ie. comparing whole nations) allow unlimited scope for interpretation. The researcher can focus on any variable over any period of time amongst infinitely varied populations. The pitfalls of using international data to make broad assumptions is so well-known that it even has its own term—the 'ecological fallacy'.

Examples of the ecological fallacy include Emile Durkheim's nineteenth century observation that suicide was more prevalent in Protestant countries[6] and the 'link', first identified in 1975, between high fat intake and higher rates of breast cancer.[7] In both cases, the statistical associations were genuine (they were, as Wilkinson and Pickett might say, too strong to be explained by chance) but the explanations given— that Protestants were more likely to kill themselves and that fatty diets caused breast cancer—were wrong. Correlation did not equal causation. Closer investigation would have shown that the suicide rate amongst Protestants was comparable to that of non-Protestants. Women who lived in countries with high-fat diets tended to give birth later or not at all, and to not breast feed— both known risk factors for breast cancer.

The Spirit Level relies on the conceit that wealthy countries are basically the same, with inequality being the main difference between them. Consequently, any disparity in social problems must be the result of inequality. This is faulty logic and a classic ecological fallacy.

It takes a peculiarly blinkered view of the world to portray Sweden, a country which has not fought a war since 1814, as being fundamentally the same as Israel, except in its distribution of wealth. Or to equate Spain and Portugal, both fascist dictatorships until the 1970s, with Belgium. Or to imagine that a culturally homogenous, traditional Asian country like Japan can only be distinguished from the United States by reference to the gap between the richest and poorest 20% of the population.

Wilkinson and Pickett conclude that if Britain adopted a Scandinavian model for its economy, it would raise levels of trust by two-thirds, mental illness would be halved, teen births would fall by a third and the murder rate would fall by 75%. In addition, they say, "everyone would have an additional year of life" and "the government could be closing prisons all over the country."

By fact-checking *The Spirit Level*, we can see that there is very little evidence to support any of these assertions. Their eye-catching life expectancy graph is based on obsolete data. The statistics they use to show an epidemic of mental illness have been carefully selected and are, in any case, based on surveys which have been widely criticised by senior psychiatrists. Only the USA has an unusually high incidence of homicide, while Britain's murder rate is lower than that of Sweden and Finland (as can be seen in *The Spirit Level*, p. 135). As for "closing prisons", that is a political decision dictated by neither economics nor, necessarily, crime.*

In the case of life expectancy, homicide, 'happiness', mental illness and obesity, there is no association with inequality whatsoever. In terms of divorce, crime, alcohol consumption, smoking, single-parent households and suicide, the more equal countries appear to do worse. For teen births and infant mortality, some English-speaking nations do worse than Japan and Scandinavia but it is very unlikely that inequality is the cause. Indeed, the two least equal countries do better than average under both criteria.

In three instances, the Scandinavian countries perform particularly well: self-reported levels of trust, foreign aid and rates of imprisonment. In each of these cases, Wilkinson and Pickett ignore important evidence that would undermine their central premise.

An ambiguous survey about trust is used as proof of social cohesion without reference to evidence (from the same survey) showing Scandinavians to be no more happy than other

---

* The only one of Wilkinson and Pickett's main criteria not tested in this book is social mobility. It would, of course, be a concern if unequal countries restrict social mobility but *The Spirit Level* graph shows just eight countries and, as its authors admit, research into this area is in its infancy. There is insufficient data to make any conclusions.

nationalities and rather less involved in community associations. Government spending on foreign aid is inappropriately used as a proxy for charitable giving and prison population is implicitly, and wrongly, used as a proxy for the crime rate.

When genuine disparities between countries are evident, Wilkinson and Pickett fail to disclose relevant information that might provide a more plausible explanation. For example, Norway is shown to do very well under most criteria but nowhere in *The Spirit Level* is there any reference to it being the world's sixth largest exporter of oil.[8] Nor is there any reference to Norway being the richest country of the 23 studied, richer even than Kuwait and Brunei.[9] In a book which contends that national wealth does not help a country 'do better', the failure to mention the billions of dollars Norway makes from oil and gas is a strange omission.

Similarly, Portugal's ban on abortion and high rate of teen marriage are more plausible explanations for its relatively high rate of teen births than the gap between rich and poor. A major factor in Sweden's relatively high life expectancy is its low rate of lung cancer, which is the result of Swedes rejecting cigarettes in favour of snus, a smokeless tobacco product which is banned in the rest of the EU. Infant mortality rates, as we have seen, are closely linked to premature and multiple births which are more common in the USA for a number of reasons which have no connection to inequality.

These are just a few examples. To list every reason why two dozen countries differ from one another would require this book to run to several weighty volumes. The omission of such crucial facts in *The Spirit Level* can only serve to mislead the reader, persuading him that the true explanation is the one Wilkinson and Pickett push so relentlessly. The omission of whole nations serves the same purpose. By showing the complete list of wealthy countries, we can see that it is not the egalitarian Nordic states that perform best but Singapore and Hong Kong, two very unequal countries of unapologetic capitalism and low taxation.

This fact alone fatally undermines the inequality hypothesis. In *The Spirit Level*, the United States is portrayed as a model of laissez-faire capitalism and the epitome of an unequal nation. This is a misrepresentation. In the Heritage Foundation's Index of Economic Freedom—as good a measure of free market capitalism as one could hope to find—Hong Kong and Singapore come first and second respectively. The United States comes eighth, below Australia, New Zealand, Ireland, Switzerland and Canada (the UK comes 11th). The notion of the USA being a land of unrestricted, unregulated capitalism is a myth.

Hong Kong and Singapore could certainly be cited as proof that economic freedom leads to greater inequality. What cannot be shown is that this inequality has led to ill-health or more social problems. If anything, the reverse is true.

The success of Hong Kong and Singapore in no way proves that inequality makes things *better*. That would be to replace one fallacious argument with another. This book has shown that more equal countries do worse under a number of criteria, but this is not to argue for greater inequality. Nor is it seriously suggested that there is direct cause-and-effect shown in any of these graphs. Equality does not 'cause' the divorce rate to rise any more than it 'causes' the infant mortality rate to fall.

We cannot rule out the possibility of some indirect effect. It is conceivable, for instance, that socialist policies are a factor in lowering aspirations and increasing the suicide rate (Wilkinson and Pickett concede that both are more common in more equal countries). It is also possible that income inequality is a factor in teen births, if combined with a welfare state and an erosion of traditional values. But in each case, there are so many more powerful factors at work that the negligible, indirect effects of inequality—if they exist at all—could never be unearthed with the blunt instrument of comparing whole nations.

Only connect

It is natural to seek a unifying trend in any set of data. This instinct is nurtured when the data is set out on a graph in a certain order with a line going through it. Take education, for example. Figure 7.1 shows combined maths, science and literacy scores for 15 year olds. A similar graph appears in *The Spirit Level*, using slightly older data.[10] Wilkinson and Pickett confidently assert that this graph shows that scores "lower in more unequal countries" and that the relationship is "strong enough for us to be sure that they are not due to chance."

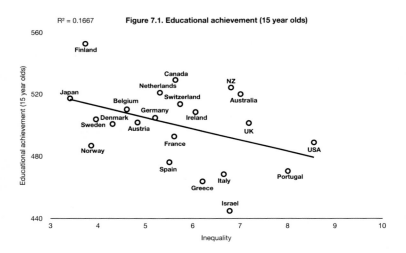

Figure 7.1. Educational achievement (15 year olds)

Perhaps so, but the countries have not been picked by chance. If we include the other wealthy countries, the correlation is much less clear (figure 7.2). In fact, a stronger correlation can be found by putting the countries in alphabetical order, thereby effectively randomising them. Data for Singapore are not available but if its educational performance is similar to Hong Kong's, as is likely, the already minimal correlation will disappear entirely. The

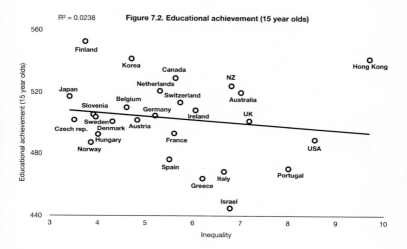

$R^2 = 0.0238$ **Figure 7.2. Educational achievement (15 year olds)**

failure to include all the relevant countries is the single biggest contributor to *The Spirit Level*'s success in showing a link between health and social problems.

The second most significant factor is the failure to seek alternative explanations, however obvious they may be. By focusing entirely on inequality, the reader becomes accustomed to thinking only in those terms.

But looking at these graphs showing educational achievement, what do we actually see? It is true that the eye is drawn to Finland's high score and the lower scores of Israel and Portugal, but is inequality responsible? If inequality is the root cause of poor educational achievement, how do we explain New Zealand's high score? If this was just one anomaly we could dismiss it as an outlier but how do we then explain why the USA, with all its different cultures and languages, gets a better score than Norway? Why is Australia doing better than Japan? Why is Britain on a par with Sweden and doing better than Denmark? When there are more outliers than inliers it is a sure sign that there is no real association.

As it happens, if there is a pattern here at all, it is geographical. Israel and the countries of Southern Europe have the lowest scores. Figure 7.3 shows the same data for educational achievement against each country's proximity to the North pole. Meaningless though this correlation is, it cannot be explained by chance.[11]

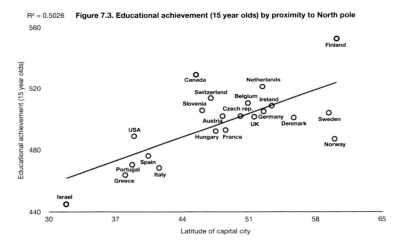

R² = 0.5026   **Figure 7.3. Educational achievement (15 year olds) by proximity to North pole**

In truth, one can find associations anywhere. The same data Wilkinson and Pickett use to make their case could be legitimately rearranged to demonstrate that teenage pregnancies are 'linked' to high rates of imprisonment, or that alcohol consumption is 'linked' to divorce (figure 7.4). No doubt there are some who would be open to such messages, but these statistical associations—strong though they are—tell us no more about the world we live in than the graphs that could be produced to show that foreign aid 'causes' theft or that recycling 'causes' suicide (figure 7.5).*

*Other graphs, showing everything from cinema attendance to women's empowerment, can be viewed at www.spiritleveldelusion.com

Our willingness to accept any of countless associations that ecological epidemiology can throw up ultimately lies in our susceptibility to the underlying message. In the case of *The Spirit Level*, a monocausal explanation for virtually every health and social problem was so appealing that the supreme improbability

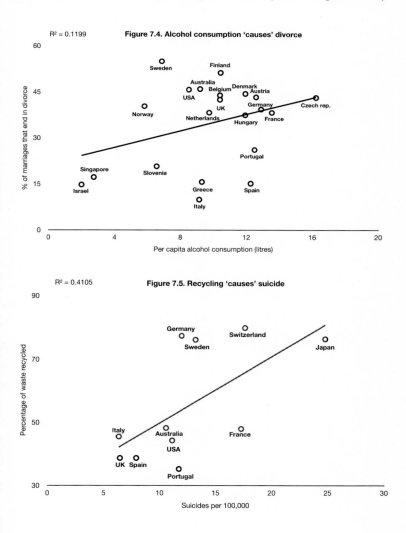

of such a grand unifying theory suddenly coming to light was cast to the back of one's mind.

The single-minded focus on income inequality requires us to ignore countless differences between countries compromising hundreds of millions of people. If we can overcome that hurdle of logic, we must take another leap of faith and believe that the widening gap between rich and poor is the single most important development of the last forty years. Seismic changes in society—the decline of religion, women's liberation, the sexual revolution, multiculturalism, individualism—must be ignored in favour of a theory of everything that rests on the population's psychological response to inequality.

But as with the Oscar winners, the truth is more mundane, less sensational and not at all newsworthy. If we ignore the inequality canard, the differences between nation states are unremarkable and unsurprising. They almost feed national stereotypes. We can see, for example, that Asian countries have low rates of crime and low rates of teen births. We can see that Scandinavians tend to be more trusting while Southern Europeans are more suspicious. We see that the wealthiest countries tend to be the happiest. We see that Americans give a lot of money to charity but that many of them are fat. The suicide rate is fairly high in Scandinavia and very high in Japan. Unemployment is rife in Spain. Singaporeans are generally law-abiding. A lot of people get killed by guns in the USA. Educational standards are higher in Northern Europe than in the South.

None of this is earth-shattering stuff and none of it goes beyond the mildly interesting unless it can be explained by some unifying theory. This, I would contend, Wilkinson and Pickett have failed to do. The dull truth is that countries do better at some things and worse at others. A lot of the time, they do much the same.

Wilkinson and Pickett are, therefore, calling for "one of the biggest transformations in human history" on the basis of evidence that is, at the very least, contradictory and inconsistent. In the name of equality, a form of political governance is being proposed that goes far beyond paying twice as much tax and adopting Scandinavian social democracy. It demands nothing less than the dismantling of the free market and an unprecedented shift of power from the individual to the state. An economic system which has, for two hundred years, produced unimagined freedom, health and prosperity is to be jettisoned in favour of rationing and state ownership. And this is all to be done in a way that cannot be reversed by future governments.

What kind of equality is this? Certainly not the equality that Alexis de Tocqueville admired in nineteenth century America. Tocqueville is cited so many times in *The Spirit Level* that the unwary reader might assume him to have been an early Marxist. In truth, it is hard to imagine anyone less likely to endorse Wilkinson and Pickett's political programme than this archetypal libertarian and life-long opponent of socialism.

Wilkinson and Pickett note that the Frenchman applauded the "equality of conditions" he observed in the United States, and so he did. He believed in the fundamental liberal values of equality before the law, the abolition of slavery and—above all—democracy. But Tocqueville never confused equality of opportunity with equality of outcome. Although the same word is used for each, their meanings are very different, as he explained in 1848:

Democracy extends the sphere of individual freedom, socialism restricts it. Democracy attaches all possible value to each man; socialism makes each man a mere agent, a mere number. Democracy and socialism have nothing in common but one word: equality. But notice the difference: while democracy seeks equality in liberty, socialism seeks equality in restraint and servitude.[12]

With remarkable foresight, Tocqueville—like his friend John Stuart Mill—predicted that a distorted definition of equality would one day lead to despotism. Liberties would not be lost overnight but would fade away incrementally.

The will of man is not shattered, but softened, bent, and guided; men are seldom forced by it to act, but they are constantly restrained from acting. Such a power does not destroy, but it prevents existence; it does not tyrannize, but it compresses, enervates, extinguishes, and stupefies a people, till each nation is reduced to nothing better than a flock of timid and industrious animals, of which the government is the shepherd.

...Thus it every day renders the exercise of the free agency of man less useful and less frequent; it circumscribes the will within a narrower range and gradually robs a man of all the uses of himself. The principle of equality has prepared men for these things; it has predisposed men to endure them and often to look on them as benefits.[13]

Apologists for Marxism have made myriad excuses for their ideology's failure to provide the same standard of living and liberty as was enjoyed in capitalist nations. Until recently, few have been so brazen as to claim that lowering living standards and curtailing freedom were the intended consequences, let alone that people would be happier with less of either. In that sense, books like *The Spirit Level* represent a departure for the left. Limiting choice, reducing wealth and lowering aspirations are now openly advocated as desirable ends in themselves.

The scale of the proposed revolution is so disproportionate to the problem it sets out to solve as to be absurd. In the final analysis, this problem amounts to what Marmot calls 'status syndrome' and what Alain de Botton calls 'status anxiety'—that we measure our status by our wealth and that, despite the trappings of affluence, we are sometimes still dissatisfied.

This is hardly a new development. Wilkinson and Pickett quote Ralph Waldo Emerson, who once wrote:

'Tis very certain that each man carries in his eye the exact indication of his rank in the immense scale of men, and we are always learning to read it.[14]

Wilkinson and Pickett cite this truism as proof that "inequality increases evaluation anxieties." A more pertinent fact, surely, is that these words were written in 1860 and long predated the consumerism and affluence of present-day capitalism.

The desire for status is not unique to modern society, nor is it even unique to human beings. Wilkinson and Pickett, along with Marmot and Layard, refer to studies of monkeys and baboons competing for status, but these studies only serve to remind us that the desire for status is innate, instinctive and inevitable. Whatever else these primates are fighting over, it is not money.

People are unequal in many ways, of which income is just one. The inequality theorists never tell us what is so special about income that makes its uneven distribution so uniquely dangerous that society needs remaking in order to afford protection. And if inequality is so damaging, why not advocate total equality? What evidence is there that those in the bottom 20% of incomes are irrevocably scarred by being eight times poorer than the richest 20%, but are happy to be four times poorer?

There is little doubt that certain possessions *do* represent status symbols for some people. Money is seen as a just reward for being talented and hard working, and while some people accumulate wealth without having either of these qualities, they represent a small minority. If we must compete for status, there are worse ways to do so than by comparing the fruits of our labour. For most of human history, status has been earned through violence, promiscuity and oppression. For centuries, rigid hierarchies meant that one's status was set at birth, according to rank and race. There may have been less status anxiety in such societies, but this should not commend them to us.

The desire to impress and attract is not inherently harmful. Status can be achieved through charity, chivalry, piety and wisdom, or it can be achieved through rape, thuggery, oppression and extortion. No matter how we go about it, the urge to stand high amongst our peers will lead to some people being perceived as being of higher status than others. If the aim of reducing financial inequality is to eliminate 'status syndrome', it is a lost cause. Even if, through a miracle of socialism, you are able to prevent people from using wealth as a barometer of success, they will find other ways—perhaps more harmful ways—of asserting their position in society.

Eliminating the symbols of prestige does nothing to address the fundamental desire for status, acceptance and respect. No political system can change human nature, though many have tried. At the most, it can only hope to shift status from the individual to the government, destroying personal liberty and aspiration as it does so. Status in the Soviet Union came from political power just as prestige came from religious power in earlier societies. Neither system was free from greed or anxiety.

The drive for equality of outcome boosts the status of politicians and bureaucrats at the expense of the individual. In its small way, Britain witnessed this after the war, as Nick Cohen has noted.

The mainstream liberal-left never wanted revolutionary socialism, but it believed in public interventionism and got it in the years after the Second World War. Status and power in the mid-twentieth century went to the men and women in the public sector who were the organizers of society.[15]

If reducing 'status anxiety' is a genuine objective, rather than a rhetorical device to push a political agenda, it is one that cannot be achieved by transferring power and prestige from one group to another. Economic freedom, at times, may lead to vanity and greed. It may also lead to disappointment and envy. But these, too, are natural human emotions that cannot be eradicated by a system of government.

If this sounds defeatist and fatalistic, it should not. It is only a recognition of the limitations of government and an acceptance of human nature. Nor should it be assumed that a little status anxiety is a bad thing, as Alain de Botton concludes in his book of the same name:

> However unpleasant anxieties about status may be, it is difficult to imagine a good life entirely free of them, for a fear that one might fail and disgrace oneself in the eyes of others is only a natural consequence of having ambitions, a preference for one set of outcomes over another and a respect for individuals besides oneself. Status anxiety is the price we pay for acknowledging a public difference between a successful and an unsuccessful life.[16]

The anti-consumerists and the inequality theorists, I would suggest, vastly exaggerate the psychological damage of these normal human emotions. In doing so, they patronise and infantilise the people they purport to be defending. Most of us come to terms with the fact that some people have more money than us at a young age, just as most teenagers come to terms with the fact that they will never be professional footballers or supermodels.

Despite the anti-consumerists' claims, we still compare ourselves to those we know and most of us set ourselves attainable and realistic goals. We might still fail, but most of us are well-adjusted enough to deal with set-backs and do not require the state either to cushion us from disappointment or lower our expectations. Sometimes we might find that the goal we set ourselves was not worth the effort, or was unattainable, but almost none of us believes we would be happier with less. Anyone who *does* feel that they are burdened with excessive affluence is, of course, free to give their money to a charity or to the treasury.

And so this book ends without a 'big idea'. If it were a scientific paper, it would be regarded as a null study, not exciting enough for publication. Its graphs do not climb spectacularly in the same direction time and again. Instead they reflect a complex world of infinite subtleties and variation. Its text offers no radical policies for transforming society, nor does it pretend that society is perfectible. It only suggests that the way forward lies in improving material conditions for all rather than forcibly protecting individuals from their own emotions.

In 2000, Dr John Lynch responded to Wilkinson's inequality hypothesis by drawing a parallel between health inequalities and airline travel. It bears repeating.

"First class passengers," he wrote, "arrive refreshed and rested, while many in economy arrive feeling a bit rough." Those fortunate enough to be in first class received the tangible benefits of comfortable seats, more leg room and better food. Most people would recognise that these material conditions made the difference between feeling refreshed and feeling rough upon arrival. Only an advocate of the psychosocial theory would say it was because the economy class passengers saw the bigger seats on their way out.

"Under a psychosocial interpretation, these health inequalities would be reduced by abolishing first class, or perhaps by mass psychotherapy to alter perceptions of relative disadvantage. From the neo-material viewpoint, health inequalities can be reduced by upgrading conditions in economy class." [17]

Nothing in history has done more to upgrade the metaphorical 'economy class' than the economic growth that consumer capitalism has brought about. More than anything else, it is wealth that has helped us to overcome the problems of the past. As for the problems of the present-day, whether we believe them to be global warming, the budget deficit, the pensions crisis or international development, there is no question that vast sums of money will be required to deal with them. These are not issues that can be solved by halting growth and redistributing whatever wealth remains.

The argument for restricting economic development must be considered suspect in any era. At a time of unprecedented national and personal debt, when millions cannot find work, let alone afford to buy a home, and at a time when we are told that we must shun cheap fuel in favour of expensive green alternatives, the argument becomes downright perverse. That it should be made by middle-class intellectuals who insist that money is not important and yet talk of little else, only adds to the sense of unreality.

Upon sober reflection, we might conclude that there is nothing mysterious about the so-called 'paradox of prosperity.' Even if we accept the view that a state of affluence does not guarantee a state of happiness, it defies reason to conclude that the answer lies in having less. A more believable explanation lies in the restlessness and ambition of the human spirit.

It should not be surprising that rising incomes lead to rising aspirations. The economist Robert Easterlin recognised this facet of human nature when he first observed the paradox of prosperity in 1974. He concluded:

Economic growth does not raise a society to some ultimate state of plenty. Rather, the growth process itself engenders ever-growing wants that lead it ever onward.[18]

Driven by a hunger for improved circumstance, society has reached unparalleled heights of happiness, health and prosperity. Pessimists and misanthropes insist that this long road of progress has come to an end. They always have. But given the choice between chasing happiness on an endless road or having our desires curbed and our horizons lowered, most of us will tolerate a little status anxiety for the freedom to keep on moving.

Notes

Notes

Introduction

(1) 'Revenge for past failings is a luxury the poor can't afford', Polly Toynbee, *The Guardian*, 4/12/09

(2) 'The way we live now' Lynsey Hanley, *The Guardian*, 14/3/09

(3) Polly Toynbee speaking at The Policy Exchange meeting 'The Future of the Left', Westminster, 18/3/10

(4) 'Books of the year', *The Guardian*, 22/11/09

(5) 'In an unequal society, we all suffer', Y. Alibhai-Brown, *The Independent*, 23/3/09

(6) 'The Spirit Level: Why more equal societies almost always do better', John Carey, *The Sunday Times*, 8/3/09

(7) 'Last among equals', *The New Statesman*, Roy Hattersley, 26/3/09

(8) In the USA, it was more modestly subtitled 'Why greater equality makes societies stronger'. The title itself remained confusing to American readers who know spirit levels as bubble levels.

(9) *Hansard*, 11/01/10

(10) *The Spirit Level: Why more equal societies almost always do better*, Richard Wilkinson & Kate Pickett, Allen Lane, 2009, p. 33; the comparison with Pasteur and Lister is made on page xi.

Methodology

(1) Unless otherwise stated, figures for gross national income (GNI) in this book come from the World Bank (2008) (http://siteresources.worldbank.org/DATASTATISTICS/Resources/GNIPC.pdf), using purchasing power parity in international dollars.

(2) 'Child wellbeing and income inequality in rich societies: ecological cross sectional study', K. Pickett & R. Wilkinson, *British Medical Journal*, 335, 1080, 16/11/07; 'The problems of relative deprivation: Why some societies do better than others', R. Wilkinson & K. Pickett, *Social Science & Medicine*, 65 (2007), pp. 1965-78

(3) For some reason, Wilkinson and Pickett use older figures for national income on page 9 than on page 7. Both graphs show South Korea, Slovenia and the Czech Republic to be richer than Portugal. Hungary is shown to be richer than Portugal on page 7 but not on page 9. Hong Kong is shown on neither.

(4) The '50 richest countries' Wilkinson and Pickett picked their final 23 from World Bank's World Development Indicators report and used data from 2002. Since the World Bank released more up-to-date figures in 2007, the authors' decision to use figures from 2002 list is odd. In international dollars, the most recent data show that Portugal has slipped out of the top 50. It sits in 59th place, with the Czech Republic in 55th place, Slovenia in 46th place and Hungary in 68th place. Using the alternative Atlas methodology, Slovenia is 47th, Portugal is 50th, the Czech Republic is 54th and Hungary is 66th. South Korea and Hong Kong are well inside the top 50, whichever measure is used. Regardless of whether they fit within Wilkinson and Pickett's somewhat arbitrary top 50 (Portugal scrapes in at 50th in the source they used), all these countries are manifestly comparable in terms of both

wealth and development. See also the UN Human Development Report 2006, p. 331 and UN Human Development Report 2009, p. 171.

(5) UN Human Development Report 2006, p. 335. As in *The Spirit Level*, I have used the average for the reporting years 2003-06 (http://www.equalitytrust.org.uk/why/evidence/methods).

1. Bad for our health?

(1) 'Survival in Academy Award-Winning Actors and Actresses', D. Redelmeiser & S. Singh, *Annals of Internal Medicine*, 134, 2001; pp. 955-62

(2) 'Income distribution and life expectancy', Richard Wilkinson, *British Medical Journal*, 18/1/92, Vol. 304; pp. 165-8

(3) 'Dear David Ennals', Richard Wilkinson, *New Society*, December 1976

(4) http://www.sochealth.co.uk/Black/black.htm

(5) *Towards Equality in Health: Income and Health*, Richard Wilkinson, Socialist Health Association, 1991

(6) 'Income distribution and life expectancy: a critical appraisal', Ken Judge, *British Medical Journal*, 1995, 311; pp. 1282-5

(7) 'Income inequality, individual income, and mortality in Danish adults: analysis of pooled data from two cohort studies', M. Osler, *British Medical Journal*, 2002, 324; p. 13

(8) 'Income, income distribution, and self-rated health in Japan: cross sectional analysis of nationally representative sample', K. Shibuya, *British Medical Journal*, 2002, 324; pp. 16-19

(9) 'Education, income inequality, and mortality: a multiple regression analysis', A. Muller, *British Medical Journal*, 2002, 324; pp. 23-25

(10) 'Social capital - is it a good investment strategy for public health?', Lynch et al., *Journal of Epidemiology and Community Health*, 2000, 54; pp. 404-408

(11) 'Poverty or income inequality as predictor of mortality: longitudinal cohort study', K. Fiscella & P. Franks, *British Medical Journal*, 1997, 314; p.1724

(12) 'Income inequality, the psychosocial environment, and health: comparisons of wealthy nations', Lynch et. al, *The Lancet*, 2001, 91; pp. 385-91

(13) 'Income distribution and life expectancy', Richard Wilkinson, *British Medical Journal*, 1992, 304; pp. 165-8

(14) 'Social capital - is it a good investment strategy for public health?', Lynch et al., *Journal of Epidemiology and Community Health*, 2000, 5; pp. 404-408

(15) *The Spirit Level*, p. 81; 'The big idea', R. Smith, *British Medical Journal,* 1996; 312: Editor's choice

(16) 'Income inequality and population health', *British Medical Journal*, Johan Mackenbach, 2002, 324; pp. 1-2

(17) 'Income inequality and mortality: importance to health of individual income, psychosocial environment, or material conditions', Lynch et al., *British Medical Journal*, 29/4/00; pp. 1200-04

Notes

(18) 'Neurohumoral Features of Myocardial Stunning Due to Sudden Emotional Stress', Wittstein et al., *New England Journal of Medicine*, Vol. 352 (6), 10/02/05; pp. 539-548

(19) 'Income inequality and mortality: importance to health of individual income, psychosocial environment, or material conditions', Lynch et al., *British Medical Journal*, 29/4/00; pp. 1200-04

(20) 'Global status report on alcohol 2004', World Health Organisation

(21) Alcohol policies in EU member states and Norway', E. Osterberg & T. Karlsson (ed.), European Commission, 2003

(22) World Development Indicators Database (http://www.nationmaster.com/graph/hea_smo_pre_mal_of_adu-health-smoking-prevalence-males-adults). The figure for Portugal comes from 1999. Figures from Greece and Hong Kong come from 2000.

(23) http://www.iotf.org/whatisiotf.asp; 'What is IOTF?'

(24) A more recent study found obesity prevalence in Sweden to be much higher, at 22.8% ('What is the accurate prevalence of obesity in Sweden in the 21st century? Methodological experiences from the Skaraborg project', Maria Nyholm et al., *Obesity*, 2008, 16 (4); pp. 896-8)

(25) 'Epidemiology of overweight and obesity in a Greek adult population: the ATTICA study', D. Panagiotakos et al., *Obesity Research*, Vol. 12, No. 12, 12/12/04; pp. 1914-20

(26) 'Validity of self-reported height and weight for measuring prevalence of obesity', N. Ashtar-Daneshi, *Open Medicine*, Col. 2, No. 3, 2008; 'A comparison of self-reported and measured height, weight and BMI in Australian adolescents', Z. Wang, *Australian and New Zealand Journal of Public Health*, 2002, 26 (5); pp. 473-8; 'The "true" prevalence of obesity', A. Kuskowska-Wolk, *Scandinavian Journal of Primary Health Care*; 1989, 7; pp. 79-82

(27) The difficulties of measuring obesity between countries cannot be overstated. The IOTF, OECD and WHO all provide very different figures. While there is no reason to believe the IOTF to be more reliable than these other organisations, their data was used in *The Spirit Level* and have been used here. The figure for Austria is strangely low (12%)—the IOTF cites a figure of 22% but states that this is 'not nationally representative'. The Canadian figure used in *The Spirit Level* (15%) is also low and comes from a self-reported survey. The IOTF's current estimate (from a 2004 survey) is used here. The IOTF's estimate for Sweden is for the town of Goteburg only and should be treated with caution. The figure for Norway should also be treated cautiously, a later study found prevalence of 18.25%, but the IOTF states that this was of a 'limited area'. Slovenia is excluded since the only available figure is self-reported. It is unclear where Wilkinson and Pickett got their higher figure for Portugal from; the ITOF consistently uses a figure of around 14%. http://www.iotf.org/database/GlobalAdultsAugust2005.asp and http://www.iotf.org/media/eco10pressrel.htm.

(28) 'The SuRF Report 2: Surveillance of chronic disease risk factors: Country-level data and comparable estimates' World Health Organisation, 2005

(29) *The Spirit Level*, p. 92

(30) Life expectancy at birth, *United Nations Human Development Report 2004*, p. 139 (data is from 2002)

(31) *The Spirit Level*, p. 7

(32) Life expectancy at birth, *United Nations Human Development Report 2006*, p. 283 (data is from 2004)

(33) Life expectancy at birth, *United Nations Human Development Report 2009*, p. 171 (data is from 2007)

(34) 'Why Cubans live longer than Americans', 28/1/10, *Big Think*, (http:// bigthink.com/ideas/18465); Cuba has a lower life expectancy in all the relevant UN Human Development Reports (2004, 2006, 2009). The figures given here are from the (most recent) 2009 report.

(35) Life expectancy at birth, *United Nations Human Development Report 2009*, p. 171 (data is from 2007)

2. Messing with our minds

(1)   ABC National Radio. Interview with Oliver James, 22/3/07

(2)   *Affluenza*, Oliver James, Vermillion, 2007, p. xiv & 237

(3)   *Affluenza*, pp. vii-xii ('Are you infected with Affluenza?')

(4)   *The Selfish Capitalist: Origins of Affluenza*, Oliver James, Vermillion, 2008, p. 4

(5)   *Unfair to Middling*, S. Lansley, TUC, 2009; 'Real compensation, 1979 to 2003: analysis from several data sources', J. R. Meisenheimer II, *Monthly Labour Review*, May 2005; pp. 3-22.

(6)   'Income inequality and the prevalence of mental illness: a preliminary international analysis', K. Pickett, R. Wilkinson and O. James, *Journal of Epidemiology and Community Health*, 60 (7), July 2006; pp. 646-7

(7)   The Canadian figure of 19.9% comes from the 2003 ICPE survey ('Mental health in Ontario: Selected findings from the Mental Health Supplement to the Ontario health survey: methodology', D. R. Offord, Toronto; Queen's Printer for Ontario, 1994). The UK figure of 23% comes from a 2001 Department of Health survey ('Psychiatric morbidity among adults living in private households, 2000: Technical report', N. Singleton, Office of National Statistics; p. 32). It unclear where the Australian figure of 23% comes from. Wilkinson and Pickett cite the 2001 Australian Health Survey, but this document doesn't mention such a figure. The 2007 Australian National Survey of Mental Health and Wellbeing does, however, give a 12 month prevalence figure of 20% (National survey of mental health: Summary of results, Australian Bureau of Statistics, 2007; p. 7). New Zealand's figure of 20.7% comes from its 2006 health survey ('Te Rau Hinengaro: the New Zealand Mental Health Survey', *Australian and New Zealand Journal of Psychiatry*, 2006, 40 (10); pp. 2581-90). The Singapore figure comes from 'Studying the Mental Health of a Nation - A Preliminary Report on a Population Survey in Singapore', C. Fones et al., *Singapore Medical Journal*, 1998, Vol. 39 (6), pp. 251-255. All other figures come from the WMH survey.

(8)   ABC National Radio. Interview with Oliver James, 22/3/07. As this quote indicates, Oliver James is dismissive of genetic explanations for human behaviour. The title of *The Selfish Capitalist* deliberately parodies Richard Dawkin's *The Selfish Gene*.

Notes

(9) 'Size and burden of mental disorders in Europe - a critical review and appraisals of 27 studies', Hans-Ulrich Wittchen, *European Neuropsychopharmacology*, 15 (2005), p. 361; 'Why does the burden of disease persist? Relating the burden of anxiety and depression to effectiveness of treatment', G. Andrews, *Bulletin of the World Health Organisation*, 2000, 78 (4); pp. 446-54; 'The epidemiology of generalized anxiety disorder in Europe', R. Lieb et al., *European Neuropsychopharmacology*, August 2005, 15(4); pp. 445-52

(10) 'Prevalence and severity of mental disorders', K. Demyttenaere et al., *Journal of the American Medical Association*, 2/6/04, Vol. 291, 21; pp. 2581-90 (To maintain scale, this graph excludes Colombia because it is a huge outlier with inequality of 25.3. WMH shows a 12 month mental illness prevalence in Colombia of 12.8%.)

(11) 'Cross-national comparisons of the prevalences and correlates of mental disorders', WHO International Consortium in Psychiatric Epidemiology, *Bulletin of the World Health Organisation*, 2000

(12) Ibid. See also 'Prevalence of psychiatric disorder in the general population: results of The Netherlands Mental Health Survey and Incidence Study (NEMESIS)', R. Biji, *Social Psychiatry and Psychiatric Epidemiology*, Dec. 1998, 33(12); pp. 587-95

(13) 'Prevalence, co-morbidity and correlates of mental disorders in the general population: results from the German Health Interview and Examination Survey' (GHS), F. Jacobi, *Psychological Medicine*, May 2004; 34(4); pp. 597-611

(14) 'Size and burden of mental disorders in Europe - a critical review and appraisals of 27 studies', Hans-Ulrich Wittchen, *European Neuropsychopharmacology*, 15 (2005), p. 357-376

(15) Demyttenaere et al., p. 2587. Dr Ronald C. Kessler, who co-directed the WMH study, accepted its limitations upon release, saying: "I'm sorry it's so fuzzy, but that's the way it is." The very low prevalence figure for Nigeria was particularly odd, since the country had suffered a great deal of ethnic violence. "It sounds like Nigeria is a paradise," said Kessler, "but I know there are camps there where lots of people have PTSD [post traumatic stress disorder]." ('Large study on mental illness finds global prevalence', Donald G. McNeil, *New York Times*, 2/6/04). The most likely explanation for the low prevalence of recorded mental illness in Nigeria and other developing countries, is that the population is largely unaware of the range of disorders that exist.

(16) As per reference (7), plus 'Mental disorders on the island of Formentera: prevalence in general population using the Schedules for Clinical Assessment in Neuropsychiatry (SCAN)', M. Roca et al., *Social Psychiatry and Psychiatric Epidemiology*, August 1999, 34(8); pp. 410-5 (Spain. Although a limited area, the authors report that their figure is "similar to those found in most studies in Spain."); 'A Norwegian psychiatric epidemiological study', E. Kringlen et al., *American Journal of Psychiatry*, 2001, 158; pp. 1091-98 (Norway); 'Prevalence of mental disorders among adults in Finland: basic results from the Mini Finland Health Survey', V. Lehtinen, *Acta Psychiatrica Scandinavica*, Vol. 81 (5), 1990, pp. 418-25 (Finland)

(17) *Affluenza*, p. 512

(18) USA: 8.7% (Vasiliadis, 2007) and 6.6% (Kessler, 2003), Canada: 8.2% (Vasiliadis, 2007) and 7.2% (Wang, 2009), Australia: 6.7% (Andrews, 2000) and 7.4%

(Hawthorne, 2008), Norway: over 7% (Ayuso-Mayeos, 2001), European average: 8.3% (Wittchen, 2005) and 8.56% (Ayuso-Mateos, 2001), Finland: 9.3% (Lindeman, 2000)

(19) Wittchen, p. 361; 'Why does the burden of disease persist? Relating the burden of anxiety and depression to effectiveness of treatment', G. Andrews, *Bulletin of the World Health Organisation*, 2000, 78 (4); pp. 446-54; 'The epidemiology of generalized anxiety disorder in Europe', R. Lieb et al., *European Neuropsychopharmacology*, August 2005, 15 (4); pp. 445-52

(20) 'The 12 month prevalence and risk factors for major depressive episode in Finland: representative sample of 5993 adults', S. Lindeman, *Acta psychiatrica Scandinavica*, 2000, 102 (3); pp. 178-84.

(21) 'Do Canada and the United States differ in prevalence of depression and utilization of services?', H. Vasiliadis, *Psychiatric Services*, January 2007, 58, pp. 63-71

(22) Ibid.

(23) Wittchen (2005)

(24) Ibid.

(25) 'A Norwegian psychiatric epidemiological study', E. Kringlen et al., *American Journal of Psychiatry*, 2001, 158; pp. 1091-98

(26) 'Prevalence of generalized anxiety disorder in general practice in Denmark, Finland, Norway, and Sweden', P. Munk-Jorgensen, *Psychiatric Services,* 57 (12), December 2006; p. 1738-44

(27) 'Depressive disorders in Europe: prevalence figures from the ODIN study', J.L. Ayuso-mateos et al., *British Journal of Psychiatry*, 2001, 179, pp. 308-16

(28) 'Prevalence, diagnosis, and treatment of depression and generalized anxiety disorder in a diverse urban community', R.C. Gwynn, *Psychiatric Services*, June 2008, Vol. 59, No 6; pp. 641-7

(29) 'Prevalence of mental disorder in an urban population in central Sweden', J. Halldin, *Acta Psychiatrica Scandinavica*, Vol. 69 (6), 1984; pp. 503-18

(30) Demyttenaere et al., p. 2588

(31) 'On being sane in insane places', D. L. Rosenhan, *Science*, 1973, Vol. 179, no. 4070; pp. 250-8

(32) 'DSM-III and the revolution in the classification of mental illness', R. Mayes & A. Horowitz, *Journal of the History of the Behavioural Sciences*, Vol. 41(3), Summer 2005; p. 263

(33) *The Trap: What Happened to Our Dreams of Freedom?*, BBC Television, 2006 (Dir: Adam Curtis)

(34) *The Loss of Sadness: How psychiatry transformed normal sorrow into depressive disorder,* A. Horwitz and J. Wakefield, OUP, 2007; p. vii-viii

(35) 'Prevalence and treatment of mental disorders, 1990 to 2003', R. Kessler, *New England Journal of Medicine*, Vol. 352 (24), June 2005; pp. 2515-23

(36) Wilkinson and Pickett are somewhat inconsistent when discussing the supposed rise in anxiety over time. On page 35, they say that: "We are not suggesting that [the rises in anxiety] were triggered by increased inequality." This is because their data show these rises to predate the rise in inequality. But on page 68 and elsewhere, they claim that anxiety is strongly related to inequality.

Notes

3. The pursuit of happiness

(1) *Happiness: Lessons from a new science*, R. Layard, Penguin, 2005; p. 228
(2) 'Does economic growth improve the human lot?', R. Easterlin, in Paul A. David and Melvin W. Reder (eds), *Nations and Households in Economic Growth: Essays in Honor of Moses Abramovitz*, New York: Academic Press, Inc., 1974.
(3) For example in 'Economic Growth and Subjective Well-Being: Reassessing the Easterlin Paradox', B. Stevenson & J.Wolfers, *Brookings Papers on Economic Activity*, Spring 2008 and 'Wealth and happiness revisited: Growing wealth of nations does go with greater happiness', M. Hagerty and R. Veenhoven, *Social Indicators Research*, vol. 64, 2003; pp. 1-27. Blanchflower and Oswald (2004) report that: "...once the British equations control for enough personal characteristics (including whether unemployed or divorced), there is some evidence of a statistically significant upward movement in well-being since the 1970s."
(4) *Happiness*, p. 125
(5) *Happiness*, p. 82
(6) World Values Survey, most recent data used in each case: www.worldvaluessurvey.org
(7) *The Spirit Level*, p. 8
(8) World Values Survey
(9) Ibid.
(10) Ibid.
(11) Ibid.
(12) Ibid.
(13) '*E Pluribus Unum*: Diversity and community in the twenty-first century. The 2006 Johan Skytte prize lecture', R. Putnam, *Scandinavian Political Studies*, Vol. 30 (2), 2007; The study concluded that "in ethnically diverse neighbourhoods residents of all races tend to 'hunker down'. Trust (even of one's own race) is lower, altruism and community cooperation rarer, friends fewer." Although such claims are often met with cries of 'racist!', this study came from Robert Putnam, America's most prominent left-wing social scientist. Wilkinson and Pickett quote from Putnam's *Bowling Alone* in *The Spirit Level* (giving the impression that Putnam believes that equality leads to social cohesion; in fact, Putnam only says that the two are not incompatible) but make no mention of his research into ethnic diversity. Aware of the potentially inflammatory nature of his conclusions, Putnam says he spent time "kicking the tyres really hard" to find alternative explanations. "People would say, 'I bet you forgot about X. There were 20 or 30 X's." After testing for many confounders, the association remained strong. ('The downside of diversity', Michael Jonas, *Boston Globe*, 5/8/07). The study was confined to communities in the USA and Putnam stressed that trust might reassert itself over time, but his findings have obvious relevance to ethnically homogenous Scandinavia when compared against multicultural nations. (I am grateful to Tim Worstall for making this observation.)
(14) *The Spirit Level*, p. 54
(15) *The Spirit Level*, p. 207
(16) 'Well-being over time in Britain and the USA', D. Blanchflower & A. Oswald, *Journal of Public Economics*, 88, July 2004

Notes

(17)'Percentage of new marriages which end in divorce, in selected countries (2002)', **Americans for Divorce Reform**. Wilkinson and Pickett do not show this correlation. Indeed, they strongly imply that the opposite is the case, talking of "the increased family breakdown and family stress in unequal countries." (*The Spirit Level*, p. 138)

(18) *League Table of Teenage Births in Rich Countries,* UNICEF, 2008; 'Monitoring ICPD Goals - Selected Indicators', United Nations Population Fund, 2009; pp. 81-84

(19) *The Spirit Level*, p. 123

(20) *League Table of Teenage Births in Rich Countries,* UNICEF, 2008; p. 5

(21) Ibid. p. 11

(22) Prior to 2007, abortion was only legal in cases of rape or if the mother's life was in danger. 'Portugal will legalise abortion', BBC News, 12.02.07. Wilkinson and Pickett's figure for Portugal comes from the pre-legalisation era.

(23) *League Table of Teenage Births in Rich Countries,* UNICEF, 2008; p. 16

(24) Ibid., p. 13

(25) Abortion rates in 2007 were 20.2, 17.0 and 0.2 per 1,000 women in Sweden, Britain and Portugal respectively (United Nations Statistics Division). Wilkinson and Pickett claim that teenagers "defer sexual activity" in more equal countries, but there is no evidence for this (p. 126, *The Spirit Level*).

(26) *An overview of child well-being in rich countries*, UNICEF, 'Percentage of young people living in single-parent families (age 11, 13 and 15)', p. 23

(27) *Happiness*, p. 67

(28) 'The Affluent Society *Revisited*' in *The Affluent Society*, John Kenneth Galbraith, Pelican, 1987; pp. xv-xvi

(29) *UN Human Development Report 2006*, p. 352

(30) 'Welfare-to-work and the new deal', Richard Layard, Centre for Economic Performance, January 2001

(31) *The Economist Intelligence Unit's quality-of-life index*, 2005

4. Crime and punishment

(1) *Ninth United Nations Survey of Crime Trends,* United Nations Office on Drugs and Crime, except Norway (2003), Belgium and New Zealand (2002), France and USA (2000) taken from *Seventh* and *Eighth UN Survey of Crime Trends*. There are no recent figures available for Austria or Greece.

(2) Several journalists mistakenly interpreted this graph as proof that unequal countries do indeed suffer from more crime; an understandable mistake that Wilkinson and Pickett do little to contradict (see, for example, David Runciman in the *London Review of Books* ('How messy it all is'), John Crece in *The Guardian* ('The Theory of Everything') and Boyd Tonkin in *The Independent* ('The Spirit Level')

(3) *Ninth United Nations Survey of Crime Trends,* United Nations Office on Drugs and Crime, 'Grand total of recorded crimes.' All figures are for 2004, except Austria, Japan and USA (2002), New Zealand, Korea and Spain (2000). Greece's most recent figure—2000—is anomalous so the 1999 figure has been used. *Seventh and Eighth UN Survey of Crime Trends*. There are no recent figures available for Australia.

Notes

(4) All figures are most recently available (2006). *Tenth United Nations Survey of Crime Trends,* except England & Wales (2005), Australia, Belgium, Hungary, Israel and Korea (2004) and USA (2002). *Eight* and *Ninth UN Survey of Crime Trends.* There is no recent data available for France.

(5) *The Burden of Crime in the EU: A comparative analysis of the European Crime and Safety Survey (EU ICS) 2005*, Jan van Dijk; pp. 106-7

(6) Ibid., p. 25

(7) Ibid., p. 39

(8) Ibid., p. 65

(9) Ibid., p. 111

(10) *Tenth United Nations Survey of Crime Trends*

(11) 'Sweden tops European rape league' *The Local*, 27/4/09

(12) *The Burden of Crime in the EU: A comparative analysis of the European Crime and Safety Survey (EU ICS) 2005*, Jan van Dijk; p. 37; Wilkinson and Pickett's only concession to this inconvenient truth is to say that: "Homicide and assaults were most closely associated with income inequality, and robbery and rape less so." (*The Spirit Level*, p. 135).

(13) *The Spirit Level*, p. 147

(14) *Prison population statistics*, Gavin Berman, House of Commons Library, 12 November 2009; p. 2; The male prison population rose from 38,040 in 1970 to 42,991 in 1993, a negligible increase when population growth is accounted for.

(15) *A century of change: Trends in UK statistics since 1900*, House of Commons Research Paper 99/111, 21 December 1999; p. 14

(16) *Crime in England and Wales 2008/09*, A. Walker (ed.), July 2009; 'Prison population statistics', SN/SG/4334; House of Commons Library; 12/11/09

(17) *Freakonomics*, S. Levitt & S. Dubner, Penguin, 2005; pp. 115-45

(18) Between 1995 and 1999, the US homicide rate fell by 28%, compared to just 4% in Canada. Europe saw its own crime rate peak in 1995. Most types of crime have declined in European countries since (Belgium is one notable exception) but more sporadically and less steeply than in the USA.

(19) *The Spirit Level*, p. 142

(20) *Crime in the United States by Volume and Rate per 100,000 Inhabitants, 1989–2008*, U.S. Department of Justice — Federal Bureau of Investigation, www.fbi.gov

(21) 'Using the P90/P10 Index to Measure U.S. Inequality Trends with Current Population Survey Data: A View from Inside the Census Bureau Vaults', R. Burkhauser et al., *Review of Income and Wealth*, March 2009, Vol. 55, Issue 1, pp. 166-85

(22) *United Nations Surveys of Crime Trends and Operations of Criminal Justice Systems, covering the period 1990-2002*, 'Total recorded intentional homicide, completed'; pp. 53-56 (eleven year average - as used in *The Spirit Level*).

(23) As Wilkinson claimed in an interview in March 2010. 'Want the good life? Your neighbors need it, too', Brooke Jarvis, *Yes Magazine*, 4/3/10. (www.yesmagazine.org) In *The Spirit Level*, Wilkinson and Pickett claim that the homicide rate is "many times higher" in the least equal countries (p. 181).

Notes

(24) *Tenth United Nations Survey of Crime Trends*, United Nations Office on Drugs and Crime. Portugal's murder rate was 1.66 and 2.15 per 100,000 in 2005 and 2006 respectively.

(25) *Black Homicide Victimization in the United States*, Violence Policy Center, January 2010; p. 2 (Data are from 2007); Wilkinson and Pickett state that there are no "ethnic disparities in rates of crimes committed" in the USA. To prove this point, they say that 25% of white Americans have committed a violent crime by the age of 17, compared to 36% of black Americans. They fail to note that this statistic shows that black youths are nearly 50% more likely to commit a violent crime (*The Spirit Level*, p. 150).

(26) *United Nations Surveys of Crime Trends and Operations of Criminal Justice Systems, covering the period 1990-2002*, 'Total recorded intentional homicide, attempted'; pp. 57-60

(27)'Suicide rates per 100,000 by country, year and sex', World Health Organisation , 2009 (http://www.who.int/mental_health/prevention/suicide_rates/en/index.html).

5. Infant mortality

(1) 'Infant mortality rate as an indicator of population health', D. Reidpath & P. Allotey, *Journal of Epidemiology and Community Health*, 2003, 57; pp. 344-346

(2) 'Income Distribution and Infant Mortality', Robert J. Waldmann, *The Quarterly Journal of Economics*, MIT Press, Vol. 107(4), 1992; pp. 1283-302

(3) 'A reply to Ken Judge: mistaken criticisms ignore overwhelming evidence', R. Wilkinson, *British Medical Journal*, Vol. 311, 11/11/98; p. 1285

(4) 'Income distribution, infant mortality, and health care expenditure', T. Tacke & R. Waldmann, Centre for Economic and International Studies, *Research Paper Series* No. 146, June 2009

(5) 'Last among equals', Roy Hattersley, *The New Statesman*, 26/3/09. It seems that Hattersley spotted that Portugal, Singapore and the USA were the only countries that were more unequal than Britain and, convinced by *The Spirit Level*'s hypothesis, simply assumed they would have higher infant mortality rates.

(6) *European Perinatal Health Report*, 2008

(7) 'Portugal slashes infant mortality rate', *The Portugal News*, 16/12/06

(8) 'World Population Prospects: The 2008 Revision', United Nations, New York, 2009

(9) 'Infant mortality in Central Europe: effects of transition', *Gaceta Sanitaria*, Vol. 20 (1), Jan/Feb 2006; pp. 63-66

(10) *The Spirit Level*, p. 184

(11)'Comparability of published perinatal mortality rates in Western Europe: the quantitative impact of differences in gestational age and birthweight criteria', W.C. Graafmans, *BJOG : an international journal of obstetrics and gynaecology*, 2001, 108(12); pp.1237-45.

(12)*Behind international rankings of infant mortality: How the United States compares with Europe*, US Department of Health and Human Services, NCHS Data Brief No. 23, November 2009; p. 5

(13)'Answers prove elusive as C-section rate rises', Rita Rubin, *USA Today*, 8/1/08

Notes

(14) 'High Percentage of Premature Births Contributing to Nation's High Infant Mortality Rate, Report Shows', Bill Hendrick, WebMD Health News, 3/11/09; http://www.webmd.com/baby/news/20091103/preemies-raise-us-infant-mortality-rate

(15) Figures for IVF use are hard to come by, but a rough estimate would be that IVF is ten times more common in the USA than in England. The USA had a rate of 236 IVF cycles per 100,000 in 2005. In 1998, there was uproar about the lack of IVF treatment in England compared to Scotland. The rate in Scotland was then said to be 21.5 per 100,000.

(16) 'The impact of the increasing number of multiple births on the rates of preterm birth and low birthweight: an international study', B. Blondel et al., *American Journal of Public Health*, August 2008, Vol. 92 (8); pp. 1323-30; 'Infant mortality statistics from the 2005 period linked birth/infant death data set', T.J. Mathews and Marian F. MacDorman, *National Vital Statistics Reports*, Vol. 57 (2), 30/7/08; p. 5

(17) 'Births: Final data for 2003', J. Martin, *National Vital Statistics Reports*, Vol. 54 (2), 8/9/05

(18) 'Epidemiology and causes of preterm birth', R. Goldenberg, *The Lancet*, 5/2/08, Vol. 371; pp. 75-84

(19) 'The differential effect of traditional risk factors on infant birthweight among Blacks and Whites in Chicago', *American Journal of Public Health*, 1990, Vol. 80; pp. 679-81; 'Familial patterns in birth characteristics: impact on individual and population risks', A. Winkvist, *International Journal of Epidemiology*, 1998 (27); pp. 248-254

(20) 'Ethnic disparity in stillbirth and infant mortality in Denmark 1981-2003', S. Fredstead Villadsen, *Journal of Epidemiology and Community Health*, 2009; 63: pp. 106-12

(21) 'Health of Children in Australia: A Snapshot', 2004-05; Australian Bureau of Statistics; 15/2/07; 'Patterns, trends, and increasing disparities in mortality for Aboriginal and non-Aboriginal infants born in Western Australia', 1980-01: populations database study', C. Jane Freemantle et al., *The Lancet*, Vol. 367 (9524); 27/5/06; pp.1758-66

(22) 'Fetal and infant deaths 2003 & 2004', New Zealand Health Information Service, D. Keylard & J. Whakaari, August 2007; 'Rates of infant mortality higher among indigenous children in Canada, the US, Australia, and New Zealand', B. Kermode-Scott, *British Medical Journal*, 338, 2/4/09; p. 1379

(23) 'Infant mortality and congenital anomalies from 1950 to 1994: an international perspective', *Journal of Epidemiology and Community Health*, 2000, Vol. 54; pp. 660-6

(24) 'Incidence of congenital anomalies among white and black live births with long-term follow-up', R. Christianson et al., *American Journal of Public Health*, 1981, 71 (1); pp. 1333-41; 'Racial disparities in mortality among infants with Dandy-Walker Syndrome', H. Salihu et al., *Journal of the National Medical Association*, Vol. 101 (5), May 2009; 'Infant mortality statistics from the 2005 period linked birth/infant death data set', T.J. Mathews and Marian F. MacDorman, *National Vital Statistics Reports*, Vol. 57 (2), 30/7/08, Centers for Disease Control

Notes

(25) 'Sudden infant death syndrome and postneonatal mortality in immigrants in England and Wales', R. Balarajan et al., *British Medical Journal*, 18/3/89, Vol. 298; pp. 716-20

(26) 'Large differences in infant mortality by ethnic group', Office for National Statistics press release, 24/6/08

(27) 'Epidemiology and causes of preterm birth', R. Goldenberg, *The Lancet*, 5/2/08, Vol. 371; pp. 75-84

6. Selfish capitalists?

(1) *The Spirit Level*, p. 60

(2) OECD, Net Official Development Assistance in 2008 (Overseas Development Aid/ Gross National Income) (http://www.oecd.org/dataoecd/25/42/42472714.pdf)

(3) 'International comparisons of charitable giving', Charities Aid Foundation, November 2006

(4) 'Charitable giving to humanitarian organizations in Spain', Arthur C. Brooks, *Hacienda Pública Española / Revista de Economía Pública*, 165, (2/2003): pp. 9-24

(5) 'Giving to charity remains high in United States', Jeffrey Thomas, America.gov, 17/6/09

(6) Private charity work in the developed world (eg. building hospitals and schools) arguably brings greater benefits than the foreign aid that is often misused or misappropriated. Dambisa Moyo makes a convincing case for viewing the whole system of aid as "an unmitigated political, economic, and humanitarian disaster for most parts of the developing world." (*Dead Aid*, 2009, p. xix)

(7) 'International comparisons of charitable giving', Charities Aid Foundation, November 2006; p. 2

(8) 'The Recycling Olympics', Planet Ark, 2004. (Average percentage recycling of paper/ cardboard, aluminium cans, glass and steel cans.)

(9) *The Spirit Level*, p. 227

(10) Kvinna inför rätta för kastad stekpanna, Sveriges Radio, Daniel Sundbaum, 8/6/08; 'The Recycling Myth', Per Bylund, von Mises Institute, 4/2/08. Bylund, a Swede now living in the USA, writes: "People are annoyed, but do not really react. Swedes generally complain a lot (about *everything*), but they do not resist; they are used to being pushed around by powerful government."

7. Ending growth

(1) Adam Smith, *The Theory of Moral Sentiments*, 1759, p. 230

(2) From 'Unto This Last' (1862); cited in *Status Anxiety*, p. 211

(3) *The Affluent Society*, J.K. Galbraith, Penguin, 1987, p. 128

(4) *The Affluent Society*, p. 127

(5) *The Spirit Level*, p. 225

(6) 'It's money that matters', *Boston Globe*, Jenna Russell, 21/2/10

(7) Adam Smith, *The Wealth of Nations*, book 5, chapter 2

Notes

(8) Estimated prevalence of compulsive buying behaviour in the United States', L. Koran, *American Journal of Psychiatry*, 2006 (163); pp. 1806-12

(9) *The Spirit Level*, p. 3

(10) *All Consuming*, Neal Lawson, Penguin, 2009, p. 60

(11) *Affluenza*, p. 75

(12) Ibid.

(13) *Austerity Britain*, David Kynaston, Bloomsbury, 2007, p. 633

(14) *Happiness*, p. 44

(15) *The Spirit Level*, p. 219

(16) *All Consuming*, p. 212

(17) Ibid., p. 211

(18) *The Spirit Level*, p. 218

(19) See also 'Bring back ration books - for booze', Janet Street-Porter, *The Independent*, 18/3/09 and 'Should we bring back rationing?' BBC website, 7/1/10

(20) 'Ration Me Up no. 1: a visit to The Ministry of Trying to Do Something About It', Andy Wimbush, NEF triple crunch blog, 29/10/09

(21) 'Ration Me Up: a message from the Minister', 20/11/09, http://thomasmatthews.com

(22) 'Bring on the recession', George Monbiot, *The Guardian*, 9/10/07

(23) 'Bring on the recession and purge our tortured souls', Tim Lott, *The Independent*, 31/8/08

(24) 'Aah, what a relief the boom has turned to bust', India Knight, *The Sunday Times*, 7/9/08. Similarly, Knight's *Sunday Times* colleague Rachel Johnson wrote an article based on the assumption that "the middle-class family has a combined income of £100,000." In fact, the median middle class family income is well under half of that. ('Haves and have-yachts', Rachel Johnson, *The Sunday Times*, 18.2.07; 'The misinterpreted middle', *The Economist*, 27/3/10, p. 27))

8. The Great Transition

(1) *The Affluent Society*, p. 71

(2) *The Affluent Society*, p. 72; Alain de Botton concurs, saying "We envy only those whom we feel ourselves to be like; we envy only members of our reference group." (*Status Anxiety*, p. 47)

(3) *The Spirit Level*, p. 222

(4) *Affluenza*, p. 42

(5) Tony Blair; interview with Jeremy Paxman, BBC *Newsnight*, 2001

(6) *The Affluent Society*, p. 73

(7) Michael Marmot, *Status Syndrome*, Bloomsbury, 2004, pp. 99-100

(8) *What's Left?*, Nick Cohen, Fourth Estate, 2007, p. 196

(9) *The Selfish Capitalist*, p. 44

(10) 'This week the average British house price is predicted to hit £200,000', *The Telegraph*, Ross Clark, 11/3/07

(11) *All Consuming*, p. 194

(12) *The Spirit Level*, p. 221

Notes

(13) *Affluenza*, p. 481

(14) *Happiness*, p. 152

(15) *Happiness*, p. 229

(16) *All Consuming*, p. 133

(17) *The Selfish Capitalist*, p. 227

(18) Ibid., p. 224

(19) Ibid., p. 210

(20) Ibid., p. 217

(21) Ibid., p. 219

(22) http://www.equalitytrust.org.uk/why/remedies

(23) *The Spirit Level*, p. 247

(24) Ibid., p. 247-8

(25) Richard Wilkinson speaking at Birkbank College, 25/4/09; http://www.youtube.com/watch?v=zEQpOXo3j34 (retrieved 26/2/10)

(26) *The Spirit Level*, p. 254

(27) *The Spirit Level*, p. 264

(28) 'Japan's gender inequality puts it to shame in world rankings', Tomoko Otake, *The Japan Times*, 24/2/08. A graph showing gender equality against inequality is shown at www.spiritleveldelusion.com. There is no association.

(29) 'Total tax revenue as percentage of GDP', OECD (2006 data) (http://www.oecd.org/dataoecd/48/27/41498733.pdf). Data for Singapore, Slovenia, Israel and Hong Kong come from the Heritage Foundation (www.heritage.org).

9. The Spirit Level fallacy

(1) 'Do Oscar Winners live longer than less successful peers? A reanalysis of the evidence', *Annals of Internal Medicine*, M. Silvestre et al., Vol. 145, no. 5, Sept. 2006; pp. 361-3

(2) 'Longevity of popes and artists between the 13th and the 19th century' (letter), M. Carrieri and D. Serraino; *International Journal of Epidemiology*, 2005; 34: pp. 1435–1444

(3) 'Statistical fallibility and the longevity of popes: William Farr meets Wilhelm Lexis', James Hanley, *International Journal of Epidemiology*, Vol. 35 (3), 2006; pp. 802-5

(4) 'Last among equals', Roy Hattersley, *The New Statesman*, 26/3/09

(5) Peter Armitage, 'Fisher, Bradford Hill, and randomization', *International Journal of Epidemiology*, 32, 2003; pp. 925-8

(6) Durkheim E 1897 *Le suicide*. F. Alcan, Paris. English translation by J A Spalding, 1951, Free Press, Collier-MacMillan, Toronto, Canada

(7) 'Experimental evidence of dietary factors and hormone-dependent cancers', *Cancer Research*, K. Carroll, 1975, 35; pp. 3374–83

(8) CIA World Factbook (https://www.cia.gov/library/publications/the-world-factbook/rankorder/2176rank.html)

(9) 'Gross national income per capita 2008, Atlas method and PPP', World Bank

Notes

(10) *The Spirit Level* uses the 2003 Programme for International Student Assessment (PISA) report and excluded the science scores. I have used the 2006 PISA report and included maths, reading and science. The general pattern remains very similar (*The Spirit Level*, p. 106)

(11) Based on the distance of each country's capital city from the North pole. Europe and North America only. This criterion is obviously, and deliberately, arbitrary and spurious.

(12) 'Tocqueville's Critique of Socialism (1848)', translated by Ronald Hamowy. Tocqueville's words cannot be attributed to a slip of the tongue or a mistranslation. He also said socialists have "a profound opposition to personal liberty and scorn for individual reason, a complete contempt for the individual", that "socialism is a new form of slavery" and that "democracy and socialism cannot go together."

(13) *Alexis de Tocqueville on Democracy, Revolution, and Society*, Alexis de Tocqueville, p. 375-6

(14) *The Spirit Level*, p. 31 and p. 44

(15) *What's Left?*, Nick Cohen, Fourth Estate, 2007, p. 194

(16) Alain de Botton, *Status Anxiety*, 2004, Hamish Hamilton, p. 302

(17) Lynch et al. 'Income inequality and mortality'

(18) 'Does economic growth improve the human lot?', Robert Easterlin, in Paul A. David and Melvin W. Reder, (eds), *Nations and Households in Economic Growth: Essays in Honor of Moses Abramovitz*, New York: Academic Press, Inc., 1974; pp. 89-121

Notes

Index

Index